Social Skills Teens Need to Survive High School

Learn to Communicate with Assertiveness to Spike Confidence, Gain Personal Growth and Squash Anxiety

M. A. Gallant

Etheria Publishing

Copyright © 2022 by M. A. Gallant

All rights reserved.

No portion of this book may be reproduced in any form without written permission from the publisher or author, except as permitted by U.S. copyright law.

This publication is designed to provide accurate and authoritative information in regard to the subject matter covered. It is sold with the understanding that neither the author nor the publisher is engaged in rendering legal, investment, accounting or other professional services. While the publisher and author have used their best efforts in preparing this book, they make no representations or warranties with respect to the accuracy or completeness of the contents of this book and specifically disclaim any implied warranties of merchantability or fitness for a particular purpose. No warranty may be created or extended by sales representatives or written sales materials. The advice and strategies contained herein may not be suitable for your situation. You should consult with a professional when appropriate. Neither the publisher nor the author shall be liable for any loss of profit or any other commercial damages, including but not limited to special, incidental, consequential, personal, or other damages.

First edition 2022

Contents

Introduction	IV
1. Stop Being Pushed Around and Become the CEO of Your Life	1
2. Who Are You... Really?	22
3. You Set the Rules	34
4. Assertiveness at Home Without a Big Blowout	53
5. Win at School - Talking to Friends, Teachers, and Foes	85
6. Getting it Done at Your Job	109
7. Dating with Assertiveness	126
Conclusion	139
Etheria Publishing Early Reviewer Program	143
References	144

Introduction

Our happiness depends on the bonds we develop with others. Digital media makes us feel connected, but it can't replace personal connection. Even those with thousands of online friends miss the satisfaction of personal contact. Many teens feel sad and lonely because of the quality of their relationships.

The communication we use online and through text messaging differs from face-to-face conversation. You might know the abbreviations and emojis necessary to write a killer text. They won't help you with personal interactions.

If we don't reply during a conversation, our friend might think we're rude. During text sessions, if you have nothing to say, it's ok not to text back. Our online friends will never know if our body language or facial expressions don't match what we say. A face-to-face conversation requires a distinct set of skills that aren't necessary with our virtual connections.

We can spend so much time online that it hinders our in-person communication. As we mature, our social skills become more important. We must interact with others at school, work, and at home without the aid of our phones. We need to learn and practice socializing to be effective in our relationships. For example, if you become employed as a hostess at a local restaurant, you'll need to be polite when welcoming visitors. While popping up on someone's phone screen with a "hey", might work online, it won't please a restaurant patron.

Those who haven't learned good communication skills may be socially awkward. This can lead to poor self-esteem. To cover, they may become a people pleaser or try to avoid personal interactions.

High school can be scary for a teen with poor social skills. The number of students between junior high and high school grows exponentially, often making you feel like a small fish in a gigantic pond. The amount of responsibility you're expected to handle also grows, ranging from a long list of assignments to having to get an after-school job. If you struggle to learn the social skills needed before you start your high school years, this might lead to other problems. Some of these issues include difficulty maintaining interpersonal relationships with friends, family, and teachers; high levels of rejection from peers; the likelihood of developing a mental illness like depression and anxiety; poor academic performance; and a higher risk of involvement in criminal acts. As you can see, if a teenager has any chance of surviving high school and graduating in one piece, strong social skills are necessary.

That's the purpose of this book, to teach fundamental social skills. Beginning with a look at who you are, what you value, and how to assert your needs. We'll discuss what assertiveness truly means and how and when to use it. You'll familiarize yourself with body language and non-verbal communication. You'll learn about setting boundaries, negotiation, and dealing with your boss. We'll also answer some important questions about dating.

Then back up our words with thirty-seven real-life examples to help you understand and practice the most important concepts.

Learning these skills will reduce anxiety, increase your confidence, and speed up your personal growth.

So, buckle up, it's gonna be a wild ride as you prepare for the rapid waves of becoming a whole new person!

I have also written a workbook to provide more practice for the exercises outlined in this book. It provides a place to write down answers to questions and has bonus content and additional practices not in this main book. The workbook is available on Amazon. You can find it here.

www.Amazon.com/dp/B0BQ99WJSC

If you have the workbook, I suggest you follow along chapter by chapter and complete the exercises.)

Chapter 1

Stop Being Pushed Around and Become the CEO of Your Life

It's not harsh to be assertive; it's harsher when people take advantage of you.

—Janna Cachola

Before we begin, it's important to ask yourself what being assertive means to you. Do you think it means to be overly aggressive to get what you want? Does it mean being difficult to deal with or rude, only thinking of yourself and disregarding everyone else's feelings? If so, then you may be the type of person most people would consider a pushover. Did you learn to stay silent about your wants and needs, to avoid making waves, and to keep your feelings to yourself? Assertiveness is essentially the equivalent of "The F-Word" for the pushovers of the world, but guess what? You can lose that title and take your power back, but first you need to learn what it means to be assertive—the correct definition.

The True Meaning of Assertiveness

Technically, assertiveness is a social skill that not only relies on effective communication but also requires you to have respect for others and how they feel. If you go by the definition, it probably sounds like what you have been doing all along, putting others and their feelings above your own, so we may need to dive a little deeper to explore the true meaning. So, let's break it down further. Someone who's assertive can communicate their needs and wants effectively while still respecting others. That sounds much better, doesn't it?

Believe it or not, it's possible to make your thoughts, feelings, opinions, needs, and wants known without appearing to be an arrogant jerk. People who are assertive don't shy away from standing their ground when someone disagrees with them or criticizes their beliefs. They're open to any critique given to them, but only if that criticism is given respectfully. Unlike a pushover, they don't lie down and take it if they are being disrespected. They also don't take hurtful comments to heart, allowing them to feel less anxiety and depression. People who are assertive can remain firm on where they stand without appearing rude.

Although this might sound like an improbable dream, it's still completely possible to accomplish. Let's find out why being assertive is important, along with the benefits of this skill.

Why Is Being Assertive So Important?

With every facet of life, mutual respect is necessary. You can't have a solid relationship, whether it be at home, work, or school, if there's a lack of respect. However, being assertive means that you also extend that respect to yourself. When you allow someone to take advantage of you, make you feel bad, or push you around, you're disrespecting yourself. The same goes for all the times you disregarded your emotions and shoved them way down because you were afraid to make someone angry with you. So, when you open your mouth and speak your mind while being respectful of the other person, you're also showing yourself the respect you deserve. That is why people who are assertive have higher self-esteem and lower stress levels.

Now, I'm not saying that if you're a pushover, then people don't respect you. I'm simply saying that even though people may respect you, you're most likely not getting the respect you deserve. Sure, they may appreciate and like you, but it's because of what you do for them. When you refuse to stand up for yourself and constantly put your own needs last on your priority list to make others happy, then you're giving their self-esteem a boost while yours suffers. You're basically telling others that their wants and needs are more important than your own. And you're sending the message that you would do anything to make them happy even if you don't intend to.

Some people like to take advantage of others who bolster their confidence and neglect their own because it's obvious that the person is an easy target. Think about it this way: if you need help, who would you rather call: the person you aren't sure would help or someone that you know would willingly drop whatever they're doing to be there for you?

You would call the latter, right? If you're a pushover, you probably have a lot more people calling you for help than to hang out.

The same thing goes for people who prefer to be more passive than assertive. Although you might think being passive and a pushover are practically the same thing, they're different. A pushover allows people to walk all over them while a passive person is easygoing and does their best to avoid conflict. Think of them as a "go-with-the-flow" type of person. While people may admire your calm demeanor, this attitude doesn't truly show that you respect yourself. When a conflict arises and a passive person just goes with whatever everyone else is saying to make life smoother, they're sending the message that their thoughts, feelings, and ideas aren't as important as everyone else's. Being passive and making yourself feel small has its own set of consequences, including but not limited to:

- high stress levels
- feeling resentment toward others
- declining mental health
- questioning yourself
- constant pressure to keep others happy

- feeling victimized

- rage

With the constant stresses of being a teenager, do you really want to add this to your repertoire of problems? I don't think so. That's why being assertive can help you out so much! Here's a list of how assertiveness can improve your life:

- an enormous boost in your confidence and self-esteem

- feeling empowered

- the ability to recognize and efficiently manage your emotions

- get the respect you deserve

- improving how you communicate with others

- better problem-solving skills

- creating strong and healthy relationships

- pride in yourself and satisfaction with your performance

So, when you compare the issues that come along with being passive or a pushover with that of being assertive, which one sounds better? Would you rather feel empowered or like a victim? Respected or taken advantage of? When you put them side by side, it's an easy decision to make, isn't it? That is why being assertive is so important. It allows you to make your feelings known and show yourself respect while communicating effectively and earning others' respect as well.

Being a "Yes Man" will not make you happy. It's the ability to say "no" when you need to that makes you feel powerful. Let's go a little more in-depth about how being assertive can lower the amount of stress and anxiety you may be feeling.

Stress and Anxiety Relief

Do you know what the biggest causes of stress and anxiety are? Poor communication! When you avoid speaking up and telling others how you are feeling or what you think, you're putting more stress on yourself. When you push your frustrations down and try to ignore them, your anxiety level is going to rise. The more you feed these two monsters, the more they will grow. Eventually, they will grow to where they boil over, and spill into every part of your life. Once this happens, you become aggressive with others. You're irritable, short-tempered, and just angry. It's when rage may make an appearance. While being aggressive, you get word vomit. So, even though you might speak your mind and let people know what you think, you're doing it at the expense of others and their feelings. This will not have the desired result and will only cause more issues.

If you had been practicing being assertive, it would have never reached this point. If you had spoken up and expressed yourself when necessary, your stress level wouldn't be as high. Using this skill allows you to have a sense of control in your life. You can control what you say, how you say it, and go into a deeper discussion if there was a misunderstanding. If you simply go along without ever speaking your mind, then you aren't fixing anything, and you won't feel good about yourself.

Taking an Active Role in Guiding Your Life

The reason many of us have so many issues with stress and anxiety and feel the desperate need to live in the virtual world is because we would rather pretend to be something we aren't rather than take control over our life. It's easier to allow someone else to be in control rather than be the CEO and take charge. Nothing good can come out of allowing others to run your life. You need to be active! To do this, you must follow the basic principles of assertiveness.

Stand Your Ground While Respecting Others

If I had to pick one sentence that I heard way too many times growing up, it must be "it's not what you say, it's how you say it." I am sure your parents have said that to you more than once, and in return, you looked at them like they were crazy. You probably even thought they were being annoying. But take a second and think about what it looks like from a different perspective.

Imagine someone who takes time out of their busy schedule to help you with something like a school project. You're extremely grateful for their help and tell them, "I know you were busy, and I really appreciate you taking the time out to give me a hand." What if they responded with "It's fine. No big deal."

Seems nice, right? If they're giving you a smile and making direct eye contact, you can assume that they acknowledge your appreciation. But what if they say those same words with a sneer, angry tone, cross their arms, and let out a loud huff? It would make you think they are feeling annoyed with you because they had to stop doing something to help you out. You wouldn't feel very good, would you?

That's why a big part of being assertive is to communicate effectively while respecting others. If your friend talked to you like that, it appears rude and disrespectful. They aren't saying how they feel and probably feel resentful toward you for disrupting their plans. They could have easily stood their ground, and said they were busy, while still being respectful. Being assertive is about thinking, acting, reacting, and communicating in a way that is both beneficial to you and to those around you.

Setting and Respecting Boundaries

Being accommodating to others is great and all, but how often do you make boundaries only to break them to appease others? I'm assuming the answer is quite often. Why do you do this? Well, because you're afraid of conflict and don't want to be seen as rude or hostile. If you set a boundary that you will not let someone mistreat you, but still allow them to do so, then they're going to think it's okay and keep treating you that way. It doesn't matter if they're your friend, parents, family members, or classmates, you must set clear boundaries and refuse to budge when someone tries to push them.

Letting people get away with treating you negatively can be detrimental to both your mental and physical health, which is why it's crucial to set personal boundaries. If you aren't sure what boundaries are, they're the limits we set for ourselves to protect us from being manipulated, taken advantage of, or mentally and physically hurt. These boundaries can include:

- when and how you would like to be touched
- letting others into your personal space
- your right to privacy
- your right to have values and opinions
- how you allow others to speak to you
- with whom you choose to be affectionate, along with when, where, and to what extent
- the right to express your personality as an individual

You may have learned these boundaries when you were younger, but as you know, teenage hormones make things go a little haywire. Besides the hormones, there are other factors like peer pressure, your reputation, and relationships with others that can play a big part in where you draw the line. However, the most important thing to remember with boundaries is that they're yours. You have every right to pull back from someone when they're dangerously close to crossing them, just like you have every right to say "no" when something doesn't feel right.

Giving Yourself Value

While gaining your self-confidence, it's also important to give yourself value. Remember that your feelings, time, opinions, and boundaries are just as important as anyone else's. You deserve to be treated with the same amount of respect and dignity as you give others. Don't allow others to mistreat you because that breaks down your personal boundaries. This also goes for you. Don't allow yourself to think that you are less important than other people, because that will only break you down and repeat the cycle you're trying to end as a pushover.

You Come First

If you're always putting off your schoolwork to help others, how is that going to help you? It's going to get you in trouble with your teachers and parents, all because you wouldn't put yourself first. Remember, your goals, priorities, and boundaries should be first before others. That does not mean you can't help a friend out if there's an emergency, but don't be afraid to put your foot down if you feel like people are calling you just because they know you will give them a hand—especially if it's not really what you want to do.

Know and Acknowledge Your Strengths and Weaknesses

Knowing what you excel at, and your list of downfalls comes in handy in instances other than job interviews. When you know your strengths, whether it be a keen eye for detail or being a team player, you can use those to your advantage. You can hone those skills and keep building upon them. The same thing goes for your weaknesses. If you know you are not good at something, like public speaking, for example, you can focus on working toward making that downfall one of your strengths.

Using the example of public speaking, you could practice giving a small speech in front of the mirror. It doesn't have to be about anything specific, maybe just a small ramble about a scene from your favorite movie. The idea is to become more comfortable practicing, and then move on to the next step, which could be practicing your speech in front of your parents. The point is a weakness doesn't have to remain a weakness. You can work on it and perfect it until the thought of facing failure no longer scares you.

It's also important to remember to take others' weaknesses and strengths into consideration as well. Everyone is struggling with something and has their own set of vulnerabilities and strengths that may be completely opposite of yours. If you recall, assertiveness requires being respectful of others; this includes their boundaries and being considerate of what skills they may be lacking.

Realize You are the One in Control

How you decide to live your life is your choice. That's one reason setting and maintaining your boundaries is so important. Nobody can tell you how to look, speak, act, feel, or think. Your parents don't get to choose what career field you go into, you do. They could influence your choices, but it's ultimately up to you.

While keeping that in mind, it's important to recognize that you don't have control over other people or what they choose to do with their lives. Just like how others may have an opinion about your life, you may have an opinion about theirs. However, your opinion doesn't get to dictate what choices they make, and vice versa.

You also cannot control how others react when you're making your wants and needs known. If they get angry because you spoke your mind, that's on them. It has nothing to do with you, and most likely has to do with their own insecurities. The way you react to others is fully within your control, though. You decide whether you're going to let others ruin your day or walk away with your head held high. Once you realize that only you have control over you, then a nice confidence boost will follow.

Choose Equality and Empathy

Being assertive is a give-and-take type of relationship. Sure, you're respecting others while respecting yourself, but you're also treating them equally and making sure you understand what they're going through. You take their point of view into consideration as they're talking to you, then you respond in a way to make sure your needs are being heard. You don't have to talk over people to be heard. Don't be rude or aggressive. Allow them to speak their mind, absorb the information, and then respond with an open and honest answer.

Owning Up to Your Responsibilities, but Still Knowing Your Limits

Since you were a young child, your parents have most likely taught you the importance of holding yourself accountable for your actions. If you broke your mother's favorite vase, you tell her what you did and make it up to her after you apologize. While assertiveness means that you stand up for yourself and speak your mind, you also need to own up to the things you have said and done. Don't cower in your room because people didn't respond well to what you did. If you made a mistake or said the wrong thing, say you're sorry (sincerely, of course) and accept the consequences so you can move forward.

People respect you more if you own up to what you did rather than trying to gaslight them and make them feel crazy because their feelings got hurt. You will also respect yourself more for holding yourself accountable rather than allowing the pressure of guilt to add to the stress you already feel.

Although, there is a limit to your accountability. Just like you have no control over others' lives, you cannot allow yourself to take on the burden of feeling responsible for what someone else did or how they feel. That was their choice. How they react is their choice. You didn't make them feel resentful or angry. They did that. Just like you hold yourself responsible for your actions, they must hold themselves accountable for theirs.

The Importance of Body Language and Non-Verbal Communication

When you're having a conversation with your friend, what are you doing with your body? Are you leaning toward them, your eyes large with intrigue, and laughing at their funny story? What about when your teacher is lecturing you about a poor grade? Are your arms crossed over your chest while you roll your eyes? Are your lips pursed in anger?

Without muttering a word, your body language is saying a lot about how you feel during a conversation. This silent form of communication may be accurate, like when you're getting in trouble (though you probably don't want to express that negative attitude). It may also send the wrong signals. You may want to hear about your friend's date, but if something distracts you, you may find it hard to concentrate. If you are looking away, fidgeting, or getting lost in your own thoughts, then your body language will betray you, hurting your friend's feelings.

To make sure you're showing the person the respect they deserve when they're talking to you and not giving them mixed signals, pay attention to these non-verbal social cues:

- *Maintain eye contact*: It can be hard and uncomfortable at first, I know, but it's an excellent skill to have. Making and maintaining eye contact, even for a few seconds at a time, lets the speaker know you're focused on them. Just try not to creep them out by staring into their eyes for too long.

- *Try not to fidget with your hands*: Fidgeting may be a way that you calm yourself down, but the person speaking might find it distracting or think you're bored with the conversation. Try to not shift in your seat, play with jewelry, pick at your nails, or look around.

- *Stand or sit up straight*: Not only is sitting and standing up straight good for your posture, but it also makes you look confident. When you slouch down in your seat or have your shoulders slumped forward, you appear defeated or self-conscious. If you want others to take you seriously, you want to appear confident—even if you aren't. Sometimes, it's a fake-it-until-you-make-it situation. However, most of the time, if you're acting like you're confident, you will feel confident as well.

- *Keep your head up*: Life is exhausting, I get it. But that's no reason to set your head down on the table when someone is talking to you. Keep your chin up, eyes focused, and show off your best qualities—your listening skills.

- *Lean in*: Moving closer to the person speaking to you shows them you're interested in what they're saying. It shows that you're attentive to their need to be heard and ensuring that they will give you the same attention.

Now that you know the importance of body language when having a discussion, it's time to learn the most effective way of saying "no" using assertiveness. I'm sure as a teenager in today's age, you've had a classmate walk up to you and say something rude or disrespectful. Maybe they're trying to embarrass you because you made them feel bad, or they're jealous of you, so they want to bring your confidence down a notch. Well, don't feel like your only choice is to stand there and take it. Without raising your voice or making yourself a doormat to their verbal abuse, you can simply end their tirade without saying a word.

Turn Away from Them

Nothing says "leave me alone and stop talking to me" like turning your back to the person trying to get a rise out of you. Remember what you read earlier: you are in control of your life and what you allow yourself to react to. If you were to react to what this person is saying and lash out at them, are you going to respect yourself afterward? Are you going to feel better about yourself, or are you going to regret lowering yourself to their level? By simply turning away from them, you're telling them that their language and attitude toward you is not worth your time.

Talk to the Hand

One of the most useful and assertive techniques to end a conversation is to put your palm out. You're telling them to stop and not to go any further. Whether it's giving yourself a second to think about your next point, so you can stand your ground, or putting up a barrier to maintain your boundaries, placing your palm out will send a message that you're in control of where the conversation goes from there.

Don't Be Afraid to Walk Away

Let's be honest, some discussions or arguments aren't worth your energy. Don't allow people to bully you into submission! Take back your control by walking away from them. This goes for every situation, whether it's at work, within your friend's group, or in a relationship. Walking away from conflict isn't a cowardly act, it's one that shows you respect yourself and your peace.

If your use of body language falls under your weakness category, you can always take the time to practice in front of the mirror. As they say, practice makes perfect! Now that you know how to take charge of your life, and how to stop being a pushover, let's get down to the nitty-gritty —figuring out who you really are.

If you have the workbook, now is a good time to review and practice what you learned in chapter 1.

Chapter 2

Who Are You... Really?

*C**onfidence is knowing who you are and not changing it a bit because of someone's version of reality is not your reality.*

–Shannon L. Adler

Just like any new skill, becoming an assertive person takes practice. However, the time, work, and patience you spend making this skill stronger will be well worth it. Within this chapter, you will learn what you need to do first to become proficient at being assertive—the art of self-reflection. This is going to help you discover who you truly are. Why do you have to look deep within yourself to discover who you are? Because you need to understand how you think and feel about yourself. This will help you to define what you love about yourself, and what you want to improve or change. This is the beginning of personal growth.

What Is Self-Reflection?

The answer to this question is simple. Self-reflection is taking the time to look deep within yourself to evaluate your thoughts, actions, behaviors, wants, needs, desires, and overall attitude. It's the question-and-answer portion of an interview, the "Why?" if you will. Then, taking the answers and breaking them down on a smaller scale to calculate where you will be headed in life if a change isn't made. It sounds complicated, I know, but it's truly not. If you think about it, it's the same process your mind goes through when you overreact to a situation and ask yourself "Why did I say those things?" and "This is what I should've said." The only difference is that you're taking that train of thought and examining every part of your life rather than just one situation.

Why Is Self-Reflection Important?

Taking the time to reflect on how you react to certain situations, such as conflicts with your parents or friends, helps you figure out new ways to become who you want to be in the world. Rather than being distracted, you place all your focus on yourself. The whole purpose of self-reflection is to take a deep look at yourself including your strengths, weaknesses, habits (both good and bad), the flaws you find in yourself, and how your choices will impact your future.

So, how does this skill benefit you? Well, it helps you to become more independent, think more rationally, learn from your mistakes, and build up your problem-solving skills. This self-reflection is required if you want to make a change in your life, which I'm assuming you do, otherwise, you wouldn't be reading this book.

Right now, you are considered a young adult because you are at a stage where you are learning to be independent, but you are not yet old enough to be fully responsible for yourself. Over the next few years, you will slowly transform into a fully independent adult; and if you don't start the process of self-reflection now, you might miss a lot of opportunities that will help you become the type of person you want to be as an adult. By looking back on the mistakes and choices you have made, you can learn from them, which will then open more doors for you.

Sure, it can sound intimidating to examine yourself piece by piece, but it does help you in the long run. Here's how:

• *A greater sense of self*: With self-reflection, you're spending your time thinking about the most important person in your life—you! It allows you to understand who you are; not who your parents, friends, teachers, or the world thinks you are.

• *Challenging yourself and your thoughts*: Your thoughts fall into one of three categories—positive, negative, and neutral. When your thoughts fall into the positive category, you feel motivated to keep going and excited for the future. However, when they're negative, you feel afraid of what the future might bring and that might stifle any initiative you're willing to make toward your goals. By self-reflecting, you can build on the positives and challenge the negatives. Are you putting off applying to a certain college because you don't want to go there and don't like their programs, or are you afraid that you might get rejected? Being afraid is never a bad thing, it keeps you moving in life, but you shouldn't let that fear dictate your life, thoughts, and choices.

•*Making decisions about your personal relationships*: Self-reflection can help you have a breakthrough when it comes to the relationships you have with others. As you think back and reflect on the past, you will come to realize who treated you with respect and who hasn't. As a teenager, much of your life revolves around your relationships whether it's with your parents, friends, romantic partners, teachers, or classmates. With that in mind, wouldn't you want your life to be better by keeping the people who are there for you, treat you respectfully, help you maintain your boundaries, and support you to stay in your life? While you dismiss the people who don't do any of those things? Think about how much better your life would be.

•*Strengthen your decision-making skills*: Part of who you are includes the decisions you make. In fact, it's a very big part. Think about it, so many things factor into the decisions you make, like your mood, attitudes, emotions, relationships, insecurities, and anyone else that the decision involves. If you don't know who you are, how can you make sound decisions that will benefit you in the long run?

- *Increase your self-awareness and inspire self-acceptance*: Becoming self-aware means that you understand and recognize your personality traits and overall emotional well-being. You know why you feel the way you're feeling at that moment and why you behave a certain way. Self-reflection and self-awareness work together because if you aren't self-aware then you can't self-reflect and vice versa. Once you're comfortable with becoming aware of who you are and where you are in life, you will slowly begin to accept yourself. Just remember that you can't skip being self-aware to bring about acceptance because you can't accept what you don't acknowledge or understand.

Quiz Time! How Would You Describe Yourself?

To discover who you are at your core and what you truly think about yourself, you must be willing to be open and honest when you describe yourself. Although this quiz won't be graded by a teacher, look over your answers when you're done and give yourself an evaluation. If you have the workbook, you can find and record your answers in chapter 2.

1. How well do you handle your emotions when you're stressed? Do you scream and fight or do you

try to figure out a solution?

2. What types of thoughts do you have when you're going to sleep at night? Positive or negative?

3. Name three things or people that make you happy.

4. Name five things about yourself that you're comfortable with.

5. Name five things about yourself that you're uncomfortable with.

6. How would you change these five things if you could? (Extra points for creativity!)

7. When was the last time you allowed someone to cross one of your boundaries?

8. What could you have done differently in that situation?

9. How do you show yourself respect?

10. In what ways do you go about working toward your goals? Are you a go-getter or are you laidback and hoping it will just happen on its own?

11. What (or who) inspires you to get up in the morning and work toward your fullest potential?

12. Are you comfortable with the way your life is going right now? If not, how would you change it?

13. Where do you see yourself in five years? Ten years? Twenty years?

14. Are the decisions you're making for your life now going to make those dreams possible?

15. Use five adjectives to correctly describe yourself. Then, ask three people how they would describe you and see how similar or different they are.

Evaluate Your Answers

Now that you have answered the questions, look them over. Are you happy with your answers? Is this how you truly see yourself? If so, I have some great news for you! You just used your self-reflection skills. Congratulations! See, it wasn't that hard, right?

The trick is to do this from time to time and compare your answers. When you can physically see the differences with your own eyes, you will notice the progress that is being made.

Understanding Your Values

In Chapter 1, you read about giving yourself value. Well, this is a different kind of value. The type of value mentioned earlier discussed the importance of showing yourself that you're worthy and don't deserve to be walked all over like a doormat.

Now, we're discussing the values that are attached to your personal ethics, ideas, and beliefs. These values regard what's meaningful to you, your life overall, and those around you. The values you have say a lot about you, like who you are, what you believe in, how you work with others, and your stance on certain topics. When you're faced with a decision, it's often your values that guide you toward the solution.

While your values can help you accomplish your goals, it's important to remember that they're not the same thing. Values don't come with a finish line, something that you can check off when you have accomplished it. Values guide you to become the person you want to be—a person you can admire and respect when you look in the mirror.

The thing is to figure out what those values are. To do this, you must look inward like you did when you were self-reflecting, but the goal is to find out what is important to you. It helps to think about times when you were the happiest and felt the most satisfied with yourself. Answer these questions to help you determine what some of your values might be:

- Think of a time in your life when you felt happy with yourself. What were you doing?

- Name two things that you are most proud of. Why do these make you feel proud?

- Are you a leader or a follower?

- Do you find it easy to forgive others when they hurt you?

- Think of a time in your life when you felt satisfied and fulfilled. What were you doing? Who were you with?

- Do you make decisions based on logic or emotion?

- How much effort are you willing to put in to achieve your goals?

- What qualities do you admire in others?

After you answer these questions, either in your head or on paper, take a second to think about your answers. These questions may have helped you identify some of your values. It might also help to look at this list and choose the 10 values that you find most important to you.

Relationships	Leadership	Generosity
Diversity	Belonging	Dependability
Creativity	Compassion	Honesty
Stability	Justice	Uniqueness
Purpose	Adventure	Positivity
Fitness	Fun	Self-Control
Challenge	Honor	Decisiveness
Intuition	Financial Security	Equality
Perfection	Preparedness	Family Oriented
Kindness	Inclusion	Hard Working

Of course, this is not a complete list of values, but it should give you an idea of what you are looking for. After you select 10 from this list, compare your list of values to your answers to the above questions. Do they seem to align?

Now, the hard part: narrow your list of values to the 5 that are the very most important to you. Needless to say, your personal values are not limited to only 5, but for now, it gives you a foundation of your highest personal principles.

What does that do for you? It helps you make decisions about things like which high school clubs to join, and what to study in college. Your choices determine the direction your life takes, and you will be a much happier person if those choices align with your values.

Here is an example: Let's say one of your top values is justice. You decide to become a lawyer because you want to help bring criminals to justice. However, right out of school the only job you can get with no experience, is being a public defender. Your first case is to defend someone who caused an accident because they were driving intoxicated. Your job is to prevent this person from being convicted if possible. If justice is of high importance to you, this job goes against your sense of right and wrong. You will probably be unhappy and may perform poorly in your job.

That is why knowing your values is crucial. They help you understand who you are so you can make choices leading you to a happy life. As you grow, your list of values might change over time, but that is ok. As you change, you will keep some and replace others that no longer serve you.

(If you have the workbook, go there now, and complete the practices for chapter 2)

Chapter 3

You Set the Rules

*A*s long as I can remember, it's been "Be a good team player, get along, follow the rules." Well, who made those rules?

–Vincent H. O'Neil

High school is a time in your life that includes many areas of conflict. Sometimes it may be within your close circle of friends, people who pretend to be your friend, bullies, your coworkers, or even your parents. Although nobody likes to argue with the people they love, or the people they don't like, for that matter, conflict is sometimes necessary. It reminds you that there's a reason you set boundaries for yourself, and it teaches you how to resolve the dispute using a reasonable and sometimes creative solution. Bringing a conflict to an end also helps you take control of your life.

Your Personal Bill of Rights

When you read the words "Bill of Rights," you probably had a flashback to your American History class as you learned about the formation of the country. If you recall, the Bill of Rights is a list of basic human rights that each of its citizens deserves; it governs their treatment. Well, a Personal Bill of Rights is similar, except it comprises the rights you give yourself regarding how you expect to be treated. It helps you maintain your boundaries and reminds you when it's time to say "no" because someone is at risk of pushing the limits you set.

If you're unsure of what a Personal Bill of Rights might look like, here are a few examples to give you an idea:

- I have the right to express myself and my emotions, even if they're negative.

- I have the right to say "no" when I feel uncomfortable with a situation.

- I have the right to change my mind without feeling guilty about it.

- I have the right to prioritize my life without the influence of others.

- I have the right to be angry with someone, even if they're a family member.

- I have the right to be silly and be myself.

- I have the right to make my own decisions about my life.

- I have the right to have my needs fulfilled, even if others don't agree with them.

- I have the right to decline an invitation without making an excuse.

- I have the right to keep my personal life private.

- I have the right to respect myself and make sure others respect me as well.

- I have the right to only maintain healthy relationships and choose to discontinue others that make me feel unsafe or uncomfortable.

- I have the right to be happy with my body, my personality, and myself.

- I have the right to love myself unconditionally and look out for my own best interests.

Now that you know what a Personal Bill of Rights should look like, I encourage you to write your own and hang it up where you can see it every day. This exercise builds up your self-worth and reminds you that set the rules for your life. You decide how you're going to let others treat you, and you decide how you're going to react when someone crosses one of your boundaries.

Your Personal Bill of Rights is essentially setting the guidelines of how you would like to be treated, and this will only make you feel stronger. However, it's critical that you know that there will be some people that don't like or appreciate your right to set boundaries. These types of people are a negative influence on your life, whether you realize it or not, and they find the fact that you're trying to change intimidating. Why would they feel challenged because you're trying to become healthier?

Because as you change and grow, you will become a more independent thinker. Your relationship with this type of person will change. You will no longer be the doormat who always gives in, and they will lose their power over you. As things develop, you realize they are not a beneficial influence in your life. This will naturally result in you pulling away from them, and the relationship may end. Asserting boundaries in your life will weed out many people who would otherwise bring you down.

What Are Boundaries and How Do You Set Them?

You read about boundaries earlier, but it's of utmost importance to learn about what they are before you try to set them. If you recall what you read during chapter 1, you set boundaries so you can protect yourself from being taken advantage of or hurt in any aspect of your life. It's the limits that you set, telling you what you will and will not allow when you're communicating with others. It's the rules that you set on how to react when someone makes you feel uncomfortable, and the ability to articulate that what they did wasn't okay. Boundaries tell the surrounding people who you are, what your values are, and how you prefer to be treated, as well as the behaviors you find acceptable and which ones you don't.

Just like everyone's Personal Bill of Rights would be different, so are everyone's boundaries. For example, you may not be a fan of personal affection, but your best friend is. So, while they don't mind giving their friends a giant hug, you may prefer to give the same people a head nod and say, "What's up?" But guess what? Both are completely fine. If both of you are happy and don't make others conform to what you prefer, then you're maintaining the boundaries that are set; that's not only showing yourself some respect but also respecting those around you.

Whether it's with your friends or with your boyfriend/girlfriend, boundaries are required to have a healthy relationship. Establishing strong boundaries allows you to have a sense of control over your life, recognize and act on your emotions, and gives you the strength to speak up when you feel like someone has crossed the line. They're also an important part of the growing-up process.

You'll find that the older you get, the more serious and influential all your relationships become, even if they're platonic, work-related, or with your classmates. Each type of relationship comes with its own set of boundaries, and all of them require honesty, respect, and healthy communication, so that we understand limits. If you don't set boundaries, it makes you more likely to fall into a dark place full of unhealthy and sometimes abusive relationships.

Although you might feel uncomfortable establishing boundaries, realize it isn't necessarily easy for anyone. It requires you to speak up when you feel disrespected and draw a line in the sand when someone keeps trying to break your personal rules. This can be extremely difficult, especially if you have spent most of your life being a pushover. But eventually, there will come a point in your life when you value your physical, emotional, and mental health over the worry of whether someone likes you.

How do you know if you have boundaries, or if they're strong enough to keep yourself safe? Let's check on how your boundaries hold up, then you can evaluate the answers and see what you may need to work on.

Boundaries Check

- What characteristics define a healthy relationship for you?

- Do you speak your mind during a conflict, or do you agree so you can avoid one?

- How often do you put the wants and needs of others over your own?

- Is it difficult to say the word "no" to people?

- Do you feel guilty or afraid when you do tell people "No"?

- How often do you say "yes" to things you don't really want to do or be a part of?

- How do you respond when someone makes you feel uncomfortable?

- Do you stand up for yourself when people mistreat you? If not, then why not?

- How many people can you honestly say you trust? Are you on that list?

- Do you make it a priority to try to "fix" others or their problems, even if it has nothing to do with you?

- How often do you do more than your share to keep a relationship going?

- Do you try to gain control over other people or allow others to control your life?

- How often do you feel comfortable expressing your feelings, thoughts, and opinions with others, regardless of whether they're positive or negative?

- How likely are you to end a relationship, platonic or romantic, if the other person keeps hurting or disrespecting you?

- Have you ever used anger or intimidation to get your way?

- How often do you allow yourself to be emotionally vulnerable (crying) in front of those you trust?

- Do you keep yourself emotionally distant from family and friends?

- Do you often worry about what your friends, family, and even parents think about you?

- Do you feel guilty about wanting some alone time to relax?

While answering these questions, make sure you're being completely honest with yourself. The whole reason for establishing boundaries is to make sure you remain safe and can live your life by your own standards. Realistically, identifying your weaknesses allows you to see where you need the strongest boundaries.

Teenagers who have difficulties establishing and maintaining boundaries often find themselves in worse trouble as life progresses. They're more likely to be in toxic relationships, have trouble deciding, and are major people pleasers. A lack of boundaries can also wreak havoc on your mental health, leaving you feeling mentally fatigued, annoyed most of the time, constantly riddled with anxiety and guilt, consumed with self-doubt, and frequently questioning who you are. Without boundaries, teens rely on being passive-aggressive to make their feelings known. Weak boundaries can also make you feel disrespected or victimized by everyone around you, but still, you prefer to stay silent because of your fear of being rejected.

Okay, we have gotten all the uncomfortable stuff out of the way. Now we can move on and learn how to set these boundaries that we have spent so much time talking about.

How to Establish Boundaries

Before we begin, just know that it can sometimes be difficult to set specific boundaries when you first start. That's because throughout the day you will go through many scenarios, and a boundary that might work for one scenario might not fit the next. But don't let that deter you the slightest bit. Setting boundaries is something that will grow along with you, and with enough practice, you will apply all scenarios to each of your developed boundaries. So, this is how you take those first crucial steps in establishing boundaries:

- *Learn how to recognize and label your many emotions*: One emotion can very well mean a multitude of things, making it much harder to figure out how you're truly feeling. For example, you become upset with your little sister for borrowing your favorite shirt, something she has done multiple times, even though you have asked her not to touch your belongings. But why are you truly upset? Are you frustrated because she never listens to you? Are you angry because she's invading your privacy and going through your things? Or are you sad because you feel like she's purposely taking your things to get under your skin, and you're feeling disrespected by her actions? Once you figure out why you're truly becoming upset, you can then use that emotion as a stepping stone toward setting your first boundary.

- *Start trusting your intuition*: There's a reason people tell you to trust your gut. Because if you feel like something is wrong, then you're probably right, and you should listen to what your "gut" is telling you. Your intuition is like your own personal Jiminy Cricket, telling you when to walk away and not get involved because the situation seems off. By listening and trusting your intuition, you're further protecting yourself and all the boundaries you have set.

- *Identify the behaviors you find unacceptable*: A major part of establishing boundaries is figuring out what actions, attitudes, and behaviors you find unacceptable, and then choosing how you would like to deal with these things when an event arises. For example, you hate that one of your friends smokes cigarettes, but you hate it even more that they're always trying to pressure you to try it. You find their complete disregard for you declining the offer to be offensive and wish they would stop. Use your friend's disrespect toward your choice as one of your boundaries and choose how to deal with their behavior when the situation happens again. Will you walk away from them? Will you tell them that until they stop with the pressure, you will not spend time with them anymore? How you choose to deal with your friend and the reaction you give them is all up to you because you make your own rules.

- *Recognize the importance of digital boundaries*: In a world of technology, it's important to remember that your boundaries shouldn't be limited to real-life situations.

Teenagers these days are notorious for cyberbullying and making the mistake of sending inappropriate photos to one another only to have it blow up in their faces. Extend the same courtesy of the boundaries you set for people you can physically be around to the people on the internet. There's a reason for the block button. You don't have to deal with any kind of harassment or people who keep trying to push your limits, and the block button makes it easy to put an end to it.

- *Learn some key phrases to help diffuse conflict*: Establishing boundaries can be difficult, but with a little practice and the use of a few keywords, you can make it much easier on yourself. These key phrases don't come without some thought though, but that's because you must figure out which works best for you to help buy some time while you mull it over. For example, if your friends invite you to a party, and you know some things will go on that you're not sure whether you would like to take part in, you could tell them, "Let me think it over, and I will let you know what I decide."

- *Remember that all relationships have limits*: You probably let your best friend get away with anything, even if their pleasure comes at your expense, right? Well, how does it make you feel when they do that? You probably don't feel thrilled about it, and their actions probably leave you feeling stressed out, right? Why do they get to be happy while you're left dealing with the consequences? That's why it's important to set limits on all your relationships. If you are everything to everybody except yourself, that isn't fair. You shouldn't allow others to dictate your happiness, so you need to draw the line on what you let them get away with. This step goes for every relationship in your life, including your parents, siblings, chemistry lab partner, etc. You must take a stand sometimes, especially if you're not the one reaping any of the benefits.

- *Practice makes perfect*: You might find this surprising, but even adults have trouble establishing and maintaining their boundaries. The reason is that they never set them when they were younger, so now they're trying to play catch-up in their later years. So, do yourself a favor and get a jump start on your boundaries now, so you aren't the adult who would rather live their life as a doormat than stand up for themselves.

When "No" Comes with Consequences

Everyone may say "No," but that doesn't mean it doesn't come with consequences when used during an inappropriate situation. For example, if your mom tells you to help her clean the house because guests are coming over, and you tell her "No," I would imagine that you're going to be in trouble. Or if you tell the boss at your after-school job "No" when they tell you to do something, you might not have that job much longer. Even telling your teacher that you don't want to do something could get you into trouble at school. If that happens, you will receive consequences from every angle.

There are appropriate times to decline a request, but sometimes using the word "No" is being defiant or downright rude. While we can still do it respectfully, it will only become effective if you use the skills already discussed earlier. Note how you can use the word "no" without appearing like a rude and defiant teenager:

- *Consider your body language*: Maintain eye contact, face the person, and make sure your facial expression matches your words and situation. A mixture of these three actions will let the other person know that you're paying attention to them while also showing them respect.

- *Pay attention to your voice and tone*: As stated earlier, it's not what you say, it's how you say it. If your boss asks you to stock shelves, what do you think the results will be if you yell "NO!"? I'm assuming it wouldn't go very well, and you would pick up your last check soon. However, if you say the same word in a very calming tone, they will know that you aren't trying to offend or disrespect them. Although you may need to use the next step to make yourself clear.

- *Know whether there should be an explanation behind the "No":* Of course, sometimes a simple "No" will suffice. Did you like the movie? No. Do you want to skip class and get drunk instead? No. Want to get fake IDs and go get tattoos? No. At other times, your "No" might need a brief explanation. Using the example of your boss asking you to stock shelves, your "No" might be more effective if you follow it up with a few more words.

You could make eye contact and tell them in a calm voice, "I'm sorry, I can't. My shift ends in two minutes, and I need to get home to work on a big project for school that's due tomorrow." Your boss may not be happy with them not having you to stock shelves, but they're more likely to be understanding because you were respectful and gave a reasonable explanation.

The Hard "No"

Circling back to the last bullet point, sometimes a hard "No" is completely acceptable. Remember, you set boundaries to protect yourself, and any situation that you feel would push your limits while going against your values shouldn't be tolerated. Understandably, saying "No" to your friends can be hard, especially if you feel like they might not like you, accept you, or could tease you about it. But keep in mind that allowing someone to pressure you into doing something you don't want to do is a sign of you disrespecting yourself. Sure, you might feel a little guilty if your friend feels hurt afterward, but that feeling will subside.

Think about this: what if you or someone else gets hurt because you went along with a behavior you didn't want to take part in to begin with? That guilt will eat away at you, and there may also be other negative consequences.

These scenarios aren't limited to your friends. They can also apply to your boyfriend or girlfriend.

Many of your friends may have paired off into couples. You may be one of those teenagers in a relationship and have taken part in some actions with your partner by now, some you may or may not be proud of. You might recall reading earlier that strong boundaries are a requirement for a healthy relationship. Regardless of how old you are, those boundaries need to be established at the beginning of your relationship with your boyfriend or girlfriend. Nobody likes to be pressured into something they aren't ready for, whether it's something simple like handholding, or more serious, like becoming sexually active.

Although your parents may not be comfortable with the subject of you becoming sexually active, the fact is that you are likely to face this issue during your high school years. More information on how to date with assertiveness is discussed later in chapter 7; however, on the topic of using a hard "no," it needs to be mentioned. You should fully know it's completely acceptable to tell your boyfriend or girlfriend "No" during your relationship. It doesn't matter how long you have been together, or how well you get along; you have every right to say "No" if you aren't comfortable with something. Even if you have done certain things with them previously and were okay with it, you're allowed to not be okay with doing them today or later in the future. As stated, many times throughout this chapter, you set the rules for yourself, and your partner should respect those rules.

Practice Saying "No" at Home

Nobody likes to feel singled out or rejected because they didn't want to do something, but don't forget that "no" gives you power and control over your life. If the very thought of saying that word makes you feel nervous, you can always practice using it with your family and friends until you become more comfortable with it.

Now, I'm not saying tell your parents "No" when they want you to clean your room because that wouldn't be effective. Instead, you could request that your mom or dad, or even your friends, make up scenarios where the word "no" is necessary. You could practice how to use it effectively in situations like when you're at work, or how to use a hard "no" when you're spending time with your friends. This is also a perfect opportunity to become more comfortable with the boundaries you set by practicing scenarios that might challenge them.

Now that you have learned how to set boundaries and become assertive outside the confines of your home, it's time to learn how to become assertive with the people you call family. This includes interacting with your siblings without feeling the need for a steel-cage match, and how to set boundaries with your Aunt Sally who's always pinching your cheeks and covering them with her bright pink lipstick every time she comes over for Thanksgiving.

(If you have the workbook, now is the time to complete the exercises for chapter 3.)

Chapter 4

Assertiveness at Home Without a Big Blowout

Raise your vibration, not your tone of voice. You gain inspiration, for peace is a choice.

–Ana Claudia Antunes

Just like any new skill, the best place to practice assertiveness is at home with the people you love and who drive you crazy the most. There are many situations where boundary setting and assertive communication can prevent conflict. One example being the situation where your younger sister keeps borrowing your belongings without asking, which was discussed in the previous chapter. The interaction that follows each discovered item she took from you might make you feel like you could just rip all her pretty hair out, especially if she ruined some things she took; but by being assertive and maintaining your boundaries, you could teach her how to do the same thing as well.

As a teenager, I'm sure it's difficult to be assertive and speak your mind when you're around your parents, maybe even your grandparents, but it's still completely necessary. The reason we needed this skill within the home is primarily because it will help you communicate with them better, leaving each person feeling heard and understood when they express their opinions, feelings, and thoughts. When everyone feels heard and respected, there's less chance that an argument will follow—especially considering misunderstandings cause most arguments.

Talking About Difficult Situations with Your Parents

If you're anything like I was during my high school years, the mere thought of talking to your parents about something serious sends shock waves through your system. Your legs get shaky, your hands become sweaty, your mouth gets dry, and your brain goes blank as you try to figure out where to start. But then you have one or two people in your close circle of friends who can openly talk to their parents about everything and anything. They go to their parents first to ask for advice and have no issues expressing their needs or wants at home.

Listening to them tell you about the relationship they have with their parents probably has you wondering, how do they do that? And is it possible to have the same type of relationship with my parents? Well, I'm here to tell you it is totally possible!

Notably, it may be uncomfortable or strange when you first talk to your parents, but it will get easier as time progresses. You might even find that you enjoy talking to them and hearing what they have to say. As a parent, I can confirm that your parents will enjoy it just as much as you do. A good heart-to-heart conversation may not begin right away, but there are some steps you can take, so you can get to that point one day.

Talk About the Small Stuff Every Day

Believe it or not, when your mom or dad asks you about your day at school, they aren't trying to pry into your personal business. They're trying to reach out and communicate with you, even if it only results in small talk. The more you talk about little things like what happened at the high school football game, how your chemistry test went, or what hairstyle you want to try next, the more comfortable you will feel when you need to talk about the big and more serious stuff.

No, you don't have to spill all the tea if you don't want to, but you could find common interests to talk about. Even if the conversation is brief, those few minutes will help create a more secure bond between you and your parents.

Find a Common Interest and Enjoy an Activity Together

Maybe you like art and so does your mom. Use this common interest and build on it. Look up art galleries or painting classes that both of you can enjoy together. It will surprise you how much easier it is to talk while you're having fun together. The activity will also give you more things to talk about, strengthening your bond, and helping you become more comfortable having a conversation with her.

There's No Such Thing as Starting Too Late

You may believe that if you have a strained relationship with your parents now, then it's destined to be this way for the rest of your life, but that couldn't be further from the truth. The relationship and bond you have with your parents is always changing, just like you are. You can choose whether you would like it to get better and put effort into strengthening it or allow it to remain as it is. It's important to know that as you get older, the problems you face, as well as the seriousness of those problems, grow along with you.

Wouldn't you much rather have someone in your corner than face your problems alone? That's one reason you shouldn't accept the state of a strained relationship, because the day will come when you need advice or help from your parents but won't know how to ask for it.

The Hard Stuff

Once you feel secure talking to your parents about the small things, the hard stuff will become much easier. In chapter 1, you learned that being assertive means voicing your wants and needs while considering the other person's feelings. When talking to your mom and dad about a difficult situation, you can use your assertive skills to move the conversation along and take it from a negative to a positive experience.

You may fear how they might react to what you're going to say, but that shouldn't hold you back from starting the conversation—especially if the topic has to do with you, your health, your future, or your safety. If you're super nervous, just know that there are some things you can do to prepare.

1. *Figure out the purpose of the discussion*: Do you have to give them some bad news? Are you asking them for their advice? Do you need help? Are you venting about a problem you're having? Are you looking for their support? Do you need their permission to do something? Are you in some type of trouble? Only when you figure out the driving force behind the discussion can you decide what

you're going to say or where to start. It will also help you figure out what you want, need, and hope to get out of the discussion.

Scenario 1

You're struggling in math and failed your last exam; you might be worried about telling them. Maybe you feel like a tutor could help you get your grades back up but aren't sure how to express this to your parents. By figuring out what you're asking them, you will know how to bring up the topic.

You could say something like, "Hey, Mom. I need to tell you about a problem I'm having in my math class. Do you think you could help me?" By clearly stating that you have a problem that needs a solution, you're also expressing your needs by asking for her help.

2. Take the time to consider how you're feeling: When you think about talking to your parents about the difficult situation you find yourself in, how do you feel? Are you terrified they're going to freak out on you? Scream, yell, or show disappointment? Are you embarrassed because the topic is extremely personal? Do you feel guilty about something you did, regardless of whether it involves your parents? Remember that being assertive means you let the other person know how you feel. Keep in mind that you're not responsible for how they react. Instead of letting your emotions take control over the situation and stop you from talking to your parents, allow your feelings to be part of the discussion—possibly using them to start off the conversation.

Scenario 2

Last night, you borrowed the car and accidentally backed into something, leaving a large dent in the bumper. You are worried that they will be angry with you. When you decide it's time to tell them (hopefully before they notice and confront you about it), you could start off the conversation with something like, "Hey, Dad, I need to talk to you. I know you might be mad, but I feel like I need to tell you, anyway. When I took the car out last night, I accidentally bumped into something, and it left a dent in the bumper. I'm truly sorry, and I will help you fix it."

Your dad might be a little angry as you predicted, but he will respect the fact that you came to him and told him the truth. It also shows him you're maturing because you're taking accountability for what you did and offering a solution to fix the mistake.

3. *Practice what you're going to say before you approach them*: Sometimes nerves can get the best of us, especially when

we're already stressed out to begin with. You might be afraid that you're going to clam up, stumble over your words, or what you have to say might come out wrong when you try to speak. Rather than worry about messing up and causing a misunderstanding that might only make the situation worse, go over what you plan to say in the privacy of your room with a trusted friend. That way, you can make sure your words, tone, and body language come across clearly and match the purpose of the conversation.

4. *Pick your opportunity to talk wisely*: make sure your parents aren't busy or are already upset about something else before approaching them. If they're already stressed out or in the middle of a task, then the likelihood of them reacting negatively, although it may be unintentional, is extremely high. Choose your time wisely by making sure your parents can focus their attention on you and put all their energy into helping you come up with a solution.

Scenario 3

You got a speeding ticket on the way home from school and will have to go to court. When you enter the house, you instantly take notice that your mom is stressed out about your younger brother misbehaving in school that day. Your dad is finishing up an important work project with a looming deadline. This might not be the best time to bring up the ticket. However, after dinner, you know your parents are in a much better mood and are more relaxed.

Even though you might be afraid of putting off the discussion by a couple of hours, it might work best to use that time to figure out what you're going to say and come up with some potential solutions. Then, even if your parents are still angry, you can show them your plan to make things right, which is sure to bring their anger down a notch or two.

(If you have the workbook, flip to chapter 4 and write what you would say in these types of scenarios.)

Effective Negotiation Skills

When you're being assertive, you're expressing your wants and needs; but what happens when your parents don't agree with what you want or need? That's when some effective negotiation skills come into play. Although negotiations can get very tricky and aren't always successful, it allows everyone involved to present their opinion and point of view on the topic. The point of negotiating is to make your feelings and opinions understood and find a middle ground where both sides can be happy with the outcome. But to do this, you must be able to communicate your points clearly and respectfully; otherwise, there won't be any happy middle ground, and you will find yourself on the losing end.

The best way to have a positive experience as you negotiate with your parents is to have a plan in place. Don't just spring the conversation on them with no warning. Tell them you would like to have a discussion with them and ask them to suggest a good time. For example, if you're hoping to get a raise in your allowance, it's probably not best to ask them as they're paying bills. Instead, figure out a time that's best for both you and them, so there are no distractions to pull anyone from the conversation. Use the time in between to plan out what you would like to say, so you can clearly state what you hope to gain out of the negotiation.

Just like when studying for a big test, make sure you do your homework. You need to bring all the evidence that helps prove your point on why you need more allowance, or why they should extend your curfew an extra hour. Think of it as a mock courtroom. If you want to affect the jury (your parents, in this case) you must have evidence to back up your claims. Show them your proposal for what you plan to buy with your allowance and how your new purchase will help you out in the long run. Or you could print off the bus schedule to show them you have a plan to get home if you can stay out later, and they won't have to pick you up. This extra step will show them there's a possibility for both sides to benefit while you openly express your intentions.

When the time comes to talk to your parents, you will want to keep your emotions in check. If you have a tantrum or start a screaming match with them, then the negotiation will fail. They will ignore any good points that you came up with while you were preparing. If you feel like the discussion is getting too overwhelming, or feel you're going to lose your cool, ask for a quick break to gather yourself and resume the conversation later.

Once you and your parents present your cases, be prepared to compromise. In a perfect world, your parents would look at all the evidence and give you the green light to do what you want, but that's not the world we live in. Even though you might feel confident about your stance and the points you have proven, there's a reason for the initial conflict. Perhaps the extra homework may have helped you out a little and given you a slight advantage, so they give in a bit, but not all the way. Maybe they extended your curfew by a half-hour instead of an hour. That's still progress. There's always a chance after you prove you can handle the new curfew and are always home on time, you could then revisit the topic later.

The last part of an effective negotiation is to ensure that you uphold your end of the bargain. Maybe your parents agreed to increase your allowance from $15 to $25 if you do a couple of extra chores a week, or they offered to pay you a few extra bucks if you watch your younger siblings that weekend while they get out of the house for a bit. By holding up your end of the bargain, you're showing that you're true to your word and increasing your parents' willingness to take part in future negotiations.

Scenario 1

You want to go to an out-of-town concert with some of your friends next weekend, but by the time you get home, it will be an hour past your curfew. You know you will have to negotiate with your parents if they're to let you go. What are the steps you will go through, and how will you present your case to your parents?

Scenario 2

The new iPhone is about to come out, and all you need to save is $150 more dollars to have enough money to buy it on the day it's released. You calculate that if your parents give you $10 more a week for your allowance, you can save enough for the phone plus tax. What are the steps you go through, and how will you present your case to your parents, so they agree to increase your allowance?

Scenario 3

For your birthday, you want to get your nose pierced. Your parents are obviously against this choice, but they allowed your older brother to get it done when he was your age. You think it's completely unfair and would like to negotiate with them, and hopefully convince them to let you do it. What are the steps you will go through, and how will you present your case to your parents?

(If you have the workbook, you can find and record how you would respond to these situations in the corresponding section of chapter 4.)

Talking to Your Parents About Your Boundaries

The relationship you have with your parents differs from all others. They brought you into this world, take care of you, taught you everything you know, and have always loved you unconditionally. So, it's difficult to bring up the subject of boundaries with them when you feel like they are crossing lines that should be respected. Maybe they feel like they're protecting you by doing certain things like reading your personal diary or searching through your bedroom when you aren't home, but you feel disrespected by what they are doing. Instances like these are when boundaries need to be established, so both sides understand what to expect.

Boundaries between parents and children have their benefits, it prevents resentment from growing on both sides. Creating a healthy bond, held together by mutual understanding and respect, supports individuality and the ability to grow. Finally, it makes the ability to communicate with each other much more comfortable. These are all long-term benefits, meaning that when you get older and eventually move out of the house, you will bring your boundaries with you. You won't have to worry about your mother dropping by randomly without calling, or your dad giving you unsolicited advice about your life and who you're dating.

You need to remember that boundaries are a two-way street. Respect their boundaries as well. That means respecting their personal space and privacy, asking before you borrow or use their things, and not relying on them for things that you can do yourself. You cannot expect someone to follow your personal rules if you keep breaking theirs.

To establish boundaries with your parents, first identify what the issue is and how it's affecting you. Here are a couple of scenarios that could help you:

Scenario 1

Recently, you discovered your mom has been reading your diary or going through your belongings when you aren't home. You feel like your privacy has been violated and that you can't trust her. You feel depressed and it's affecting your relationship with her. How do you approach her about the situation? What do you say to her?

To be heard, you must be open with your parents about how it makes you feel when they keep pushing or disregarding the boundaries you have set. You will want to remain calm and try not to argue when bringing up the subject, as an argument will only make matters worse.

Scenario 2

Every weekend, your parents expect you to babysit your younger siblings, even when you want to make plans with your friends. You were okay with it when you were younger, but now you're getting upset that you never get to do anything with your friends or go on dates. How do you bring up the subject with them?

One way you could do this is by telling them, "While I enjoy watching my brother and sister, and I realize that you two should have some alone time together, I feel like I am at an age when I should be allowed time to spend with my friends or go on dates as well." This example shows that you have respect for your parents' need to spend time together without the stress of children, but also your needs are not being met when you're expected to stay home every weekend.

If you have the workbook, you can find and record how you would respond to these situations in chapter 4.

Establishing boundaries with your parents can be hard, especially when you know that they're doing these things out of love. But by doing so, everyone will feel heard, understood, and it will help improve your overall relationship.

Dealing With Your Siblings

Brothers and sisters have a special way of pushing your buttons, unlike anyone else, right? You love them to death, but sometimes they make you feel like if you're in the same room as them for one more second, you might lose your mind. The back and forth can be exhausting, like an emotional rollercoaster. They push your boundaries, but only because they know which nerve to push to get a reaction out of you.

My brother used to get me in trouble for yelling at him in the car because he would keep his finger an inch away from my face and do the old "I'm not touching you" gag. Siblings can be merciless and the fact that you live under the same roof as them only makes it worse because you see them every day. However, it doesn't have to be this way forever.

Remember what you learned earlier. You cannot control other people, but you can control how you react to them and their behavior. Even if your brothers or sisters are the most annoying, ungrateful, and disrespectful people in the world, you can change the tides by how you act toward them and hope they make the change on their own. Here are a few tips on how to deal with your siblings when they just keep pushing your limits without losing your cool:

• *Look over your Personal Bill of Rights*: Reminding yourself of the rules you set will help you recall how you wish to be treated. Your Personal Bill of Rights doesn't just apply to how you want your friends and the people outside your home to treat you. It also applies to your family members, including your pesky little sister who likes to blare "SpongeBob SquarePants" on the television at 6 a.m. every Saturday.

• *Establish some boundaries with them*: This is the time to draw that invisible line in the sand. Sit them down and have a calm and rational one-on-one conversation with them. Nobody likes to be embarrassed, so telling them about these boundaries during a family dinner might just start an argument and make you look vengeful by calling them out in front of everyone. While you're alone with them, tell them what they're doing that you find unacceptable. Then, tell them what the consequences will be if they keep violating those boundaries.

Scenario 1

This one is for the little sister who likes to wake you up with the loud television. You could sit her down and tell her, "Look, I know you like to watch cartoons when you wake up in the morning, but you always wake me up when you turn the TV up all the way. I wake up early every morning for school, so when you do that and ignore me when I ask you to turn it down, it feels like you're disrespecting me and my need for sleep. If you continue to do this, I will not take you to the park to hang out anymore for our one-on-one time. If you can't respect me, then I'm not spending extra time with you."

- *Mentally prepare yourself for some pushback*: It may take time for your siblings to take your boundaries seriously. If you're like most siblings, you have probably threatened them with some type of consequence on more than one occasion when they were on your nerves. So, for a while, your brother or sister might take your consequences as an empty threat and try to call your bluff. Be ready for the push back but stay consistent with maintaining your boundaries and follow through with the consequences.

Scenario 2

Suppose your older brother seems to believe that the family car is his to use at his disposal. He never refills the gas tank when he uses it, leaving you to buy all the gas. You might find yourself extremely frustrated with him.

After sitting him down to talk about it and telling him you will no longer fill the gas tank if you weren't the last one to use it, he's most likely going to continue to bring the car back on empty. In that case, when you use the car, only put enough gas in the tank to replace what you used. He will soon learn his lesson when he's running late for work and the tank is empty because he didn't want to listen to you or respect your boundaries.

You might feel guilty about him getting in trouble at work, but if you don't stand your ground, then you will just be enabling him. He needs to learn responsibility and not rely on you to bail him out, meaning you are not responsible for his choices or actions and are still fulfilling your Personal Bill of Rights.

Think before you react: Every time you interact with someone, you're left with a variety of emotions. You could feel angry, happy, sad, mentally exhausted, etc. It all depends on how the person behaves or what they do when they're around you. Siblings are no different. Often, I would have a great time hanging out with my brother or sister and feel happy with how the day went. Other times, I was so mentally exhausted because they constantly annoyed me with their worst behavior. Many times, you may snap at your siblings if they're teasing you, pushing your buttons, and being downright obnoxious, but acting that way isn't doing anything but adding fuel to the fire. They know they're getting under your skin, so as any brother or sister does, they're going to keep pushing until you give them a bigger reaction. Do not feed into it! Take a second to think of a more effective and rational way to deal with them. If talking to them in a calm voice and telling them how they're pushing your boundaries doesn't work, and they refuse to listen, remember what you learned in chapter 1 when you read about non-verbal body language. You may walk away or turn your back on them. You don't have to stay in the same room as them and continue to be disrespected.

- *Recognize your triggers and don't be afraid to respond appropriately*: We all have triggers that bring up certain emotions. Certain TV shows might make you happy because they bring up happy memories of hanging out with your best friend. Certain songs might make you upset because the last time you heard them, you were going through a difficult breakup. Unfortunately, because you live in the same house as your siblings, they're very aware of what buttons to push to get a certain reaction, and they may even enjoy getting you worked up. If you have had a conversation with them, maybe on multiple occasions, and they constantly keep triggering you, then it's your right to respond appropriately and remove yourself from the situation.

Scenario 3

Your older brother and sister both know that you feel insecure about your height but like to get a rise out of you by calling you a nickname like "Shorty" or "Tiny". They're purposely triggering you. Sadly, they're teasing you despite knowing your insecurity. You have respectfully told them many times to not call you those nicknames and how you feel when they do it, but they continue because they know it gets you upset. It is understandable that you feel disrespected because they keep ignoring your wishes. You may feel angry and frustrated with them.

If you can't seem to get through to them about what they're doing to you, then it's time to remove yourself from the situation. Get up and leave the room and stick with the consequence you told them you would enact if they kept teasing you. Maybe you told them you would no longer spend time with them if they kept calling you names, so follow through with it. Obviously, it's hard to avoid them when you live in the same house, but whenever you're in the same room and they call you names, get up and leave. Don't subject yourself to their disrespect or else they will keep doing it.

- *Remind yourself that this is a temporary problem*: Sure, siblings are forever, but living with them isn't. That means you only have a few more years until one of you moves out. Once you're living separately from them, it will be up to you when and how often you interact with them. You have control over your life now, but you will have even more control when you're out on your own. If they continue pushing your boundaries and breaking your rules, you can choose whether you move forward in your relationship with them. You don't have to answer their phone calls, text messages, or visit them if every interaction you have with them leaves you feeling angry, upset, or mentally exhausted.

We all want a healthy relationship with our siblings. Bickering, teasing, and even shouting matches with our brothers and sisters are a normal part of this relationship, to a degree. These interactions play a huge role in our personal development. It is how we learn people skills and conflict resolution. Most of the time, siblings are close friends for life despite the arguments that happen between them while growing up. 10, 15, or 20 years from now, your relationship with your siblings will be nothing like they are today.

Unfortunately, sometimes it doesn't work out that way. If this is the case and they spend their adult life still pushing your boundaries and disrespecting you, then you have every right to decide how you respond to their treatment. You may decide that you can only be around them at family gatherings. Worse case, you may decide to cut them out of your life entirely.

During your high school years, it's best to use your assertiveness and boundary-setting skills to the fullest while waiting to see how the future of your relationships unfold.

Being Assertive with Other Adult Family Members

Dealing with the people you live with is one thing, but it's a whole other ballgame with family members you only see on holidays and at family events. We all have people we're related to that when we hear they're going to be attending a gathering, we immediately start looking for the nearest exit. Those are family members who always violate your personal space, ask prying questions about your personal life, embarrass you without regard for your feelings, and give you unsolicited advice about what you should do with your life.

Maybe they're the type to just drop by without calling or are constantly asking you to borrow money, clothes, or for a ride. They're needy and can't take a hint that you want them to leave you alone. Unfortunately, these types of relatives often lack self-awareness and can't realize how much of a burden their actions are on the people they love. The only way you will deal with them is by using assertiveness. Here are a few steps on how you can get through life with boundary-crossing family members:

- *Don't bother trying to fix them*: People are usually set in their ways, especially if they're in their later years of life. It's not like a child or a pet that you can train, and as you learned earlier, it's not your job to fix people. All you can do is accept them as they are and respond appropriately. The good news is unless there are some type of unforeseen circumstances, you don't live with these relatives. Choose how much you would like to interact with them.

Don't answer their phone calls or help them if you don't want to. You can choose not to attend the same events as them or stand around and socialize with them. You have every right to get up and leave if they keep pushing your limits. Sure, you could talk to them and explain the issue, but if they continue acting or behaving in a way you find unacceptable, you don't have to keep trying to make the relationship work.

- *Stay present in the situation*: If a family member who likes to push your boundaries is around, your body may send you all kinds of signals to abort the mission. Your blood pressure might go up a little, your heartbeat quickens, and you begin feeling anxious, which can throw you into fight-or-flight mode. While understandable, try to avoid giving this person the benefit of a reaction. Fight-or-flight mode is a defense mechanism, and when in that state, you can become defensive about anything they say or do which could lead to an argument. Keep yourself grounded in the present moment by controlling your breathing or other grounding techniques. If you must interact with them, be assertive with every subject you talk about, making sure you say what you mean and mean what you say. Keep your focus on how you respond, and if the conversation turns into a conflict, express your feelings, and subtract yourself from the equation.

- *Watch for triggers*: As discussed with siblings, relatives know your triggers if they know you well enough. Sometimes they may do it unintentionally, especially if you don't spend time with them that often, but it's bound to happen with a difficult family member. If they don't know what a certain topic triggers for you, then pull them aside and have a conversation with them, letting them know how you feel about it.

Scenario 1

It's a couple of months before you graduate, and you're becoming increasingly anxious about which major to choose for college, and your know-it-all aunt keeps bringing it up. Every time she mentions it causes you to feel more anxiety, and you decide to have a little talk with her.

You could say something like, "I know that you're trying to help me pick what career I should go into, but I'm already stressed out enough about my choice. If you could please avoid talking about it, I would appreciate it." By telling her this way, you're not only speaking to her respectively, but you're also letting her know how her actions are making you feel and telling her your needs. If she continues to talk about it and completely disregards what you said, then you have every right to end the conversation and walk away.

- *Keep certain topics off-limits*: Usually when someone asks you an embarrassing question, you might find the urge to pay them back and do the same to them. But this may not be the best solution to the problem. You may have topics about your life that you prefer to keep to yourself, and that's perfectly normal. There are things about my private life that I wouldn't want my grandma or even my mother to ask about. But if you have one of those relatives that are relentlessly hitting you with questions that you find embarrassing and won't stop, it might be time to have a conversation with them about their unacceptable behavior.

Scenario 2

Your grandma always brings up your social life or who you're dating, and you might feel uncomfortable. Maybe you're in a new relationship and aren't sure whether it's serious. Or maybe you're single and not ready for a relationship yet. Either way, it's not your grandma's business, nor is it okay for her to pry into your personal life. Even though she's most likely doing it out of love and just wants you to be happy, it isn't her place to ask questions or give advice.

You could sit her down and say something like, "Grandma, I know you're looking out for me and want to make sure I'm happy, but please don't ask me questions about my personal life. When you do this, I feel embarrassed and uncomfortable. If the time comes, when I feel comfortable telling you this information, I will."

- *Maintain your physical boundaries*: We all show our affection for others in different ways. Some people may love to hug and kiss their loved ones while others prefer a simple hell0 and to stay in their own little bubble. Both are acceptable and normal because those are the boundaries we have set for ourselves. However, there always seems to be that one relative that's way too hands-on and likes to insert themselves into everyone's personal space. Nothing makes you feel more uncomfortable than unwanted affection, and these types of family members have yet to realize the impact they have on people when they act this way. Even when you ask them to stop, they try to make you feel guilty for not wanting their affection, which only makes you feel worse. If this happens, despite your warning about not wanting hugs and kisses, express yourself to them, and tell them what's on your mind.

Scenario 3

Your uncle is a loving person and likes to give hugs way too much, making you feel you should keep your distance. You don't mind having a conversation with him, but he always seems to get right into your personal space. This makes you feel uncomfortable, and you try to back away, but he doesn't take the hint and gets right back into your bubble. You love your uncle because he's funny and a nice person, but his lack of respect for your personal boundaries is disrupting your ability to be around him.

Talk to him alone and say something like, "I know that you're an affectionate person, and while I love giving you a hug when I first see you, I feel uncomfortable when you invade my space. Please respect my personal space." Now that he knows your boundary, it's up to him how he reacts to it. He could either abide by your wishes and keep a safe distance from you, so you can continue having a healthy relationship, or he can ignore them and not get to spend time with you at all.

DNA doesn't mean that they're allowed to trample all over your boundaries. If they want to continue having a relationship with you, then they should respect you, just like you would expect from a friend or coworker. Yes, blood is thicker than water, but a relationship with your family isn't free. It comes at a cost: mutual respect, honesty, communication, and trust. Without those four things, you may as well be strangers.

With the bases covered at home, we can now move on to the place you love to hate—high school. When you start school your freshman year, the building looks so big and wondrous—but you soon realize that the place can be torture if you lack the social skills to adapt. So, let's dig in and learn how you can deal with your classmates, teachers, and even enemies using assertiveness.

(If you have the workbook, it's time to flip to chapter 4 and do the exercises for this chapter. You will find all the scenarios from this book, as well as some extra ways to practice assertiveness.)

If you are enjoying this book, it would make my day if you left a review. Scan this QR Code

or go to

https://www.amazon.com/review/create-review/?ie=UTF8&channel=glance-detail&asin=B0BQ99WJSC

Find All of Our Books at:

www.EtheriaPublishing.com

Chapter 5

Win at School - Talking to Friends, Teachers, and Foes

*B*e calm; yet assertive. Be meek; yet courageous. Be gentle; yet bold. Be kind; yet strong.

–Charles F Glassman

Your high school years may seem like they will last forever, but they fly by faster than you realize. Although you enter the school as a bright-eyed and bushy-tailed ninth grader, dreaming about what could happen in the halls during those 48 months, the changes you will experience can easily catch you off guard. Not only will the homework be much harder than the year before, but you will notice a change in your friends. Sometimes, you will stay close and finish out the time together, but there's also a chance you may go your separate paths or even become mortal enemies.

High school is stressful by itself, but if you're lacking the social skills to help you interact with others, it can easily fill those four years with conflict. To get through these years in one piece, you must learn to navigate all the challenges of maintaining relationships with friends; dealing with other kids who may not like you or bully you; and effectively communicating with teachers and other school officials. It might sound scary, especially if you have spent much of your life keeping to yourself, but high school is like a jungle. The only way you will survive is to be prepared.

Using Assertiveness with Your Friends

How we communicate with our friends differs from how we communicate with our parents, siblings, coworkers, bosses, and teachers. We tell them our secrets, joke around with them, maybe even tease each other a little, or play harmless pranks on one another. If it's all in good fun, no harm done, right? But what do you do when your friends become a source of stress for you? The answer is you tell them what's on your mind. Friendships, like any relationship, require mutual respect, honesty, loyalty, and trust for them to last for a long time. However, if you let your friends single you out, walk all over you, or make you the punchline of every joke, how are you going to maintain a strong friendship or your mental health?

If the time comes, when you're not sure where you stand in your social circle, ask yourself this question: "What qualities make a person a good friend?" Then, compare those qualities with the ones your friends are exhibiting.

- Do they support you?

- Are they respectful of your boundaries?

- Can you trust them?

- Do they make you feel good about yourself or do they make you feel bad about yourself?

- Are these the characteristics that you want to be associated with?

- How do you feel when you're around them?

Although it seems like a tall order to fill, it's not when your mental, physical, and emotional health is on the line. Friends are supposed to help build you up, not cut the cords to your parachute and laugh as you crash to the ground. That's why being assertive with your friends is so important. You must let them know how you expect to be treated if they want to remain a part of your life.

What Would You Do?

Let's work out some likely scenarios you might come across in your group of friends and think about how you would react to them. There are no wrong answers, but it will give you the opportunity to use what you have learned so far about being assertive and apply them to the situation.

Scenario 1

You sit with the same group of friends every day during lunch. You used to enjoy laughing and talking to them, but recently one of your friends has begun talking over you. Anytime you try to get a word in, they cut you off, and you don't understand why. After a couple of weeks, they continue to do this, but you have yet to speak up because you don't want to lose your friends or make them angry with you. So, you continue to sit in silence and stop trying to contribute to the conversation. Recently, you noticed that whenever it's almost lunchtime, you start to feel angry and are ready to explode. As you sit there and eat lunch, the friend who has so rudely been cutting you off asks you what's wrong. What do you say to them?

If you use the assertive skills you have read about so far, you might say something like, "I would appreciate it if you didn't talk over me. It makes me feel disrespected and seems like you're intentionally doing it to hurt my feelings. If you continue treating me this way, I'm going to find another table to sit at." By stating your response this way, you're telling your friend what you find unacceptable (talking over you), what you need from them (wanting them to stop), how it makes you feel (disrespected), and what will happen if they continue to act this way (finding a new group of people to sit with).

Scenario 2

You and your friend always take turns picking what you want to do on the weekend, and usually, it ends up being something you both enjoy. However, this weekend your friend wants to go to the movies and see a new film that you have already seen and hated. You try to make excuses about why you don't want to go, but they're persistent about going to see the movie. When you tell them you don't want to see the movie, it only makes your friend mad at you. What do you say to them?

If you're being assertive, you might say something like, "I understand that you really want to see the movie, but I told you I have already seen it and didn't like it. I still want to spend time with you and hang out, so maybe we could come up with a compromise. We could do something that we both want to do; Or if you still want to see the movie, then you can go, and I will do something else. We can just hang out some other time."

Just like the previous scenario, you're openly stating how you feel (not wanting to go to the movie), what you want (to do something you both enjoy), and what will happen if they decide to do their own thing (doing something else and hanging out on a different day). Except this scenario is a little different because you added the possibility of a compromise, so you could come up with a decision together. You left the choice in their hands, but they know what will happen depending on what they choose. You can't control their choice, but they know the options and consequences of each one.

Scenario 3

Your best friend tells you about a party at a hotel that they want to go to, but you know your parents won't let you go because there won't be any adults there to supervise. Your friend tells you to just sneak out because they really want to go to the party. It's always the biggest party of the year. If you don't show up, then you will be a nobody for the rest of your time in high school. You want to go but know that if your parents found out that you snuck out and went to a party you will face serious consequences. Also, you know that there will be drinking and smoking at the party, and there's always a chance that the police will be called, and it has happened before. If that were to happen, you could also face legal consequences. Your best friend keeps begging you to go, and you know they will be mad at you if you don't agree.

What do you say to them?

Noting the consequences, you could face if you go along with the plan to sneak out and using the assertive skills you have learned so far, you might say something like, "I know you want to go to this party, but I don't want to. I understand if you're mad at me for my decision, but it's not worth getting in trouble with my parents if I get caught sneaking out. Plus, the cops get called on this party sometimes, and I don't want to have a criminal record that could ruin my chances of getting into college. If you still want to go to the party, that's your choice. But I'm not going."

With this scenario, you're stating all the same objectives as before, but you're also reminding your friend of the consequences they might face if they decide to go to the party. This could help them make the right decision once they take a second to weigh the pros and cons of going while stating your position clearly and respectfully.

There aren't any wrong answers. Everyone expresses themself differently. It's just how you express yourself that matters. If you're doing it with confidence, openness, honesty, and respect, then you did it right. You're being assertive.

I understand how hard it can be to stand up to your friends, especially when there's a possibility of losing them. However, if they're your genuine friends, they will understand and respect your decision. But with fake friends, bullies, and frenemies, it might get a little difficult. They have already proven that your opinion and feelings don't matter to them. So, how can you deal with them without becoming a doormat for their aggressive behavior?

Let's find out together!

How to Handle Bullies and Fake Friends

If you have seen any movie about high school, you know that the main character always has enemies, whether it's a bully or a couple of fake friends. The real high school experience isn't much different but lacks the comedic element, especially when you're the one being picked on. Standing up to the person who's making every day a living nightmare probably sounds terrifying to you because you do not know how they're going to react. Are they going to get angry? Will their bullying get worse? Will they just give up and walk away?

To make matters worse, there are various kinds of bullies. There are ones who are overly aggressive and use violence to terrorize others. Then, there are the people who use manipulation, humiliation, and intimidation tactics to control their victims (Think Regina George and the Plastics from Mean Girls). Nobody really knows what drives bullies to behave the way they do, we can only speculate it has something to do with a lack of self-esteem and confidence, unmet needs, or a poor home life. They use their insecurities as a driving force to hurt others and make their victims feel bad, so they can feel better.

So, how do you deal with bullies and people who don't like you? Here are a few tips on how you can handle them:

- *Display your confidence*: Bullies and manipulative people have the ability to pick up on others' insecurities. They watch you and figure out what makes you tick, and then target that shortcoming mercilessly. However, on the off chance that they choose to single you out, do you know what's going to stop them? Stand up to them, but in the right way. My parents always taught me that if you resort to yelling or calling names during an argument with someone, you already lost. Although I didn't understand it back then, as I got older and dealt with difficult situations, it finally clicked. You don't have to lower yourself to their level to get them to back off. By speaking to them with confidence and expressing how you feel about their treatment of you, they will realize that they will not get the reaction that they're craving. Do not feed the monster!

- *Remember you have rights*: The Personal Bill of Rights that you wrote can come in handy here. Whether it's with a person claiming to be your friend or someone bullying you, there's nothing forcing you to stand there and take it. If the person is supposed to be your friend and keeps trying to break you down, then you need to re-evaluate that relationship. You have the right to spend time with people who support, respect, and treat you fairly. Nobody has a right to trample on those boundaries or make you feel less than.

- *Focus on how you respond to them*: Being passive or passive-aggressive with people who are intentionally trying to harass you isn't the best option. It only allows them to up the ante and shows them they're getting to you, which is what they want. Rather than using an emotionally charged tone when approached by a bully, speak in an emotionless and flat tone with direct language. By removing your feelings from your voice, you're depriving them of any joy they get out of your reaction. It tells them you have no intention of becoming their victim.

- *Make your body language a weapon*: Words aren't enough to get someone to leave you alone. Body language reinforces what you're saying to those that wish to do you harm. Think back on what you learned in chapter 1. Even if your words and tone are strong, if your shoulders slump over or you don't maintain eye contact, then the disconnect is going to be seen as a weakness. Stand up straight, exude confidence, make eye contact, say your piece, and walk away.

- *There's no shame in asking for help*: I was a teenager once, and I know no one likes a "snitch." However, with your safety, all bets are off. You shouldn't have to suffer in silence because there's nothing to be ashamed of. If you don't feel comfortable talking to an adult, tell a couple of friends you trust. They can have your back whenever you're being picked on, and strength comes in numbers. Bullies prefer to deal with people they think are weaker than them, so a few friends supporting you will certainly help.

Because teens deal with fake and difficult friends often, we will start with some scenarios on how to deal with them first.

(If you have the workbook, you can find and record how you would respond to these situations in chapter 5.)

Scenario 1

Although you and another teen hang out in the same friend circle, you have a feeling that they don't like you very much. On more than one occasion, you have overheard them making fun of the way you dress and your physical appearance. Even though you expect your friends to stand up for you, they say nothing at all and laugh at the hurtful remarks made about you instead. This hurts your feelings, but you don't want to say anything and start trouble. But one day, you decide enough is enough and decide to confront this person about their comments. What do you say to them?

An assertive teen would choose to confront the person the very next time they overhear negative comments being made. You would want to use your best body language, look confident, and in front of the group say, "I don't appreciate the way you talk about me when you think I am not around. I have overheard you making fun of me several times and I find it rude and hurtful. It makes me feel you are not a friend at all, even though you say nothing like that to my face."

Here, you have stated your position when it can't be denied by the person who is out of line, but you are giving them, and your other friends, a chance to respond before making any ultimatum. Their response will help you decide if you continue to be friends with any of these people, or if you give them a chance to make amends.

Scenario 2

One of your close friends is a fairly athletic person. Whenever they laugh or say hello, they punch you in the arm. Although they don't mean to hurt you, it hurts because they do it so often. You wish they would stop, and even though they apologize and say they will stop, they continue to do so. After talking to them about their hitting again, they do it the next day, so you decide to change your approach when you speak to them. What do you say to them?

In this scenario, the friend isn't necessarily a fake friend, but they seem to lack boundaries. To make your point about how their hitting is affecting you, it might help if you said something like, "Please stop punching me. I have asked you to stop multiple times, but you keep doing it. Not only does it hurt when you hit me, but it shows that you don't respect my boundaries or my feelings. If you do it one more time, I will not hang out with you anymore."

As you can see, by saying this, you're telling them how their actions affect you both physically and mentally, while telling them what will happen if they continue to act this way.

Scenario 3

Recently you have noticed that one of your friends has become extremely combative, not only with you, but with everyone. They feel the need to argue with anything someone says. If you were to say the sky is beautiful and clear that day, they would point out the one dark cloud. You aren't sure what's going on with them as they refuse to talk about it and only act defensive when you bring their behavior up. One day, they're in a bad mood and start a stupid argument over something small. What do you say to them?

This scenario might be difficult because it's obvious that your friend is going through some tough times, possibly at home or elsewhere. Taking their feelings into consideration, it might be helpful to say something like, "You seem to be going through something that you obviously don't want to talk about, but your constant need to argue with everyone is making it hard to enjoy spending time with you. If you would like to talk to me privately about what's going on, I don't mind hearing about your problems, but I don't enjoy being treated like a punching bag. It's frustrating and makes me feel mentally drained when I argue with you about everything."

Even though it might sound a little harsh, being direct and getting to the point might be the only way to get through to this person. However, by telling them you're there for them if they would like to talk in private, you're reminding them you're there to support them, but aren't willing to put up their combative behavior. You also told them how their unacceptable actions are affecting you.

With bullies, they may be a little trickier to deal with, but if you stick with the tips given above, then these scenarios could be exactly what you're looking for.

Scenario 1

While you're talking to one of your friends in the hallway, you accidentally mess up your words and stutter a bit. Another student passes by and hears you, and instead of walking by, they mock you. The other student isn't a stranger to you. In fact, they have openly mocked and teased you many times. Previously, you had ignored them and hoped they would leave you alone, but that doesn't seem to work. It seems to happen more often. Since they don't get the hint that you don't think them mocking you is funny, you decide to stand up for yourself and confront them. What do you say to them?

Whether they're trying to be funny or cruel, this person obviously doesn't care about your feelings or else they wouldn't continue to mock you even after you ignored them. When you confront them, it would work best if you used a calm and unemotional voice. You don't want them to get that reaction from you as you say something like this, "I'm sure you think that you're being funny, but your behavior is frankly just distasteful and immature." Then, you turn your back on them, letting them know that the conversation is over.

Again, yes, it sounds a little harsh, but the language is direct. You let them know how you perceive their behavior to be unacceptable. Last, you turned your back on them, which concluded the discussion. Although the bully won't be happy about you standing up for yourself, they will realize that you're unwilling to be a victim of their ridicule. A bully can't thrive off someone standing up for themselves because that would be too much work. They need a victim that will stay quiet and act like a doormat, which is what you were doing before when you ignored them.

Scenario 2

Your ex-partner is in a new relationship, and their new partner seems to have a problem with you. Not only have they spread malicious rumors about you around the school, but they have also sent copies of all the private text messages between you and your ex to everyone you know and posted them on social media, tagging you in every post. Now, everyone in your grade has teased you about the embarrassing things you wrote to your ex. How do you handle this situation?

Unfortunately, this type of situation happens all too often in today's society and there aren't any winners. The ex's new partner is most likely jealous of you for whatever reason and has their own insecurities about themselves, which fuels the smear campaign against you. This scenario might work best if you get some help from your parents or even from the school.

Scenario 3

One day, you make the mistake of saying something about one of your classmates, and through the high school grapevine, your words eventually reach the person. Of course, by the time the person heard what you said, it's completely misconstrued and made much worse than it was. Feeling disrespected by the misunderstanding, the person challenges you to a fight. What do you do in this situation?

Scenarios like this can escalate quickly, and it might seem difficult to gain control over the situation, especially if the person is extremely angry. However, you could try to regain control by saying something like, "I can understand why you're angry, because you feel disrespected by what you believe I said about you. However, I will not fight you. If you would like to talk about this civilly and solve the issue, then we can do that instead." Hopefully, with a calm tone and making eye contact, you can de-escalate the situation, but as you have learned, you cannot control others.

If your friend calms down and agrees to have a conversation about what you did, then be ready to give a genuine apology for talking about them. If things continue to escalate and they do become physically threatening, you have every right to defend yourself from physical harm.

Scenario 4

This one's for gamers, as a lot of bullying in high school, takes place online. You and your friends are playing a multiplayer game online when a new player joins the game. Almost immediately, the new player spews hateful slurs toward you and your friends and even goes as far as continuing their tirade in the private chat. Every message they send is worse than the last. How do you handle this situation?

This is a trick question. Think back to chapter 3, where we discussed digital boundaries. The best way to deal with this situation is to hit the block button. They created it for a reason after all and that was so people like the new player don't ruin the activity you take part in to relax and have fun.

Another big part of high school is the interaction you have with teachers.

Although communicating with school officials may seem intimidating at first, it's important to remember that they're human, just like you. They expect to be shown respect by the students and return the same respect they're given. So, let's figure out how you can use your newfound skills of assertiveness with your teachers.

How to Be Assertive with Your Teachers

The way you interact with your teachers, principals, and other school officials may make or break your time in high school. They're usually the ones who give you recommendations when the time comes to apply to colleges, and a good impression goes a long way with them. How you communicate with them and behave in their class can determine whether you're going to get an extension on your term paper, or if you're going to be spending most of your four years in detention. Regardless, being assertive can go a long way with your teachers.

Teachers are human, and there will be days when they aren't in the best mood. They might be a little snippy with their students, and this can make it harder to communicate with them effectively. While you should still be respectful when you speak to them, just know that you have every right to stand up for yourself if there is a misunderstanding that needs to be resolved. Here are a few scenarios about being assertive with your teachers:

Scenario 1

Your history teacher assigned you a research paper last week, and you worked very hard to fulfill every requirement the assignment needed. You finished the paper on time and turned it in and spent the last few days feeling anxious about getting the assignment back to find out how you did. When you get the paper back today, you're upset to see that you got a poor grade on it. You look the paper over but don't see why you got so many points off. You approach your teacher after class, ready to ask them about your grade. What do you say to your teacher in this situation?

In this situation, you would handle it just as you would when you approach your parents to talk to them. Make sure you maintain eye contact, and even though you aren't feeling great because of the poor grade, keep an upright posture. You want to appear confident in your work, so slumped shoulders won't be of any help. Say something like this, "Mr. So-and-so, I was hoping we could discuss my grade. I worked very hard on this paper and triple-checked it to make sure I covered everything needed in the requirements, but I still received a bad grade. Could you tell me what I did wrong, so I know for next time?"

By going this route, you're showing the teacher that you care about your grade. The words appear confident if used with a tone that matches and shows by stating how hard you worked on the assignment that you weren't slacking off and didn't rush to get it done. Teachers like to see students trying their best, and even if you didn't do well on one assignment, asking what you did wrong, so you don't make the same mistake next time, will show them you're trying. That initiative, along with your confidence and assertiveness, might be just what you need for them to offer you some extra credit, or for them to allow you to redo your paper.

Scenario 2

During math class, your teacher hands out a unit test and tells everyone to keep their eyes on their own paper. While finishing up the last few questions, the person in front of you drops their pencil, grabbing your attention. You look up at the student, and your teacher thinks that you're trying to cheat off their paper. The teacher takes your test and gives you detention. After class, you decide to speak with the teacher and plead your case. What do you say to the teacher to get them to realize they made the wrong assumption?

For this and the last scenario, you probably noticed that it started by approaching the teacher after class. The reason for this is that if you do this during class, in front of everyone, the teacher might think you're trying to be defiant. Plus, they have twenty-something other students they're trying to teach, so speaking to them during the time they should be teaching isn't the best option. They won't be thrilled to stop their lesson to focus all their attention on you. However, in this scenario, you might feel humiliated because they accused you of cheating. Reacting irrationally won't help you prove you did nothing wrong.

Instead, it would work best if, like last time, you maintain eye contact and have your body language match your words. You could say something like, "I understand why you thought I was cheating, but it's not what you think. The person in front of me distracted me so I looked up. I'm not the type of person to cheat on a test, especially when I studied for two hours last night to make sure I was ready. I would like you to reconsider my consequence because I wasn't cheating."

By saying this, you're giving your teacher the facts and showing them you can see why, from their perspective, it looked like you were cheating. If you have never caused an issue in their class, they might believe you, but it's essentially up to the teacher. You can't control how they will react to your words, but you can control how you react to their response. Life can be unfair, and it's possible that you will still end up in detention. However, you stood your ground and let your feelings be known about the situation. Sometimes, that's all you can do.

Now that you have learned how to deal with teachers, you can learn to communicate with the next person in charge of your future—your boss.

(It's time to go to the workbook and do the practice exercises for chapter 5)

Chapter 6

Getting it Done at Your Job

*D*on't think for a moment that you've gotta be perfect to be paid.

–Clifford Cohen

Even as a teen, a part-time job can come with challenges. These may include conflict with coworkers, your boss, and sometimes rude customers. There may be days when a difficult customer pushes all your buttons to no end, your boss is on your case about everything you do, and all your coworkers are being childish. You feel you might lose it if you don't handle it correctly. Assertiveness techniques can be useful in job situations, helping you to keep your cool when conflicts arise, and keep you from losing your job.

Using Assertiveness to Get the Job

The whole job search process can be overwhelming and stressful. You must find places that work with your school schedule, figure out how you can get to and from work if you don't have a license, fill out the application, and keep your fingers crossed until you hear from the company. When you finally get the call requesting an interview, you will probably feel even more stressed out by answering the questions correctly to get the position.

Luckily, most of the questions will probably be like the ones you asked yourself during the self-reflection process. All you need to do is make sure your body language matches your tone and words to bring the interview home.

Some common questions you might hear during the interview include:

- Why do you want to work here?
- Can you tell me a bit about yourself?
- Can you work weekends?
- What are some of your strengths and weaknesses?
- Do you have reliable transportation?
- If we're short-staffed, are you able to come in on short notice?

If you're nervous about how you may come across during the interview, the best thing you can do to prepare is practice with one of your parents or a friend. You could do a mock interview and allow them to give you feedback regarding what you need to work on.

Many employers aren't looking for specific answers to their questions. When you answer, they watch your body language to see how confident you are. They observe if you maintain eye contact, your posture, if you're fidgeting, and if you seem genuinely interested in getting the job or seem forced to apply. They want someone who truly wants to be there, so you want to make sure the message that you do comes across loud and clear.

You might have varied responses pertaining to your work schedule. For example, if you're active in sports, there might be some conflicts in your schedule on weekends. So, during the interview, when the employer asks you if you can work weekends, you could say, "I can't work every weekend due to practice or games, but if I'm needed, I can come in to work the morning (or night) shifts on those days." Companies that hire high schoolers are used to working around the obligations of students, so you should be able to work something out.

Another example could be if you don't have a driver's license but live relatively close to the business, you could answer the question about reliable transportation in this way, "I won't have my license for a few more months, but I only live a few blocks away. I have no issue walking to work until I'm able to drive." Both answers show that you're ready and willing to show up to work, on time, and really want the job. With the combination of confidence, using the correct body language, and straightforward answers, you will be more likely to get the job over the other nervous teenagers who didn't prepare.

(You can find and prepare your answers in chapter 6 of the workbook. Then use those answers to practice for your interview.)

Dealing With Your Boss

Like your parents, your boss's job is to keep you on track and redirect you when you do something incorrectly. Don't worry when this happens because it's common in every work environment. The best way to handle this is by accepting responsibility for your actions and holding yourself accountable when you're wrong, just like you learned in chapter 1.

When your boss is trying to tell you the correct way to do something or is criticizing your work, don't get defensive and think they're singling you out. Everyone goes through a training stage, and they're teaching or telling you these things to make sure your shift runs smoothly. It's best to acknowledge your boss' criticism and try to think of it as a teaching moment. There may be times you might not agree with everything they're saying, and you can do so respectfully and with the use of the assertive skills you have learned so far.

Let's go over a couple of scenarios about how to handle a conflict with your employer and write how you would react to them in the workbook.

Scenario 1

You got your first job at an ice cream shop and have just started training. The first few days of training were hard, and you made a lot of mistakes, but you think you're finally getting the hang of it. A customer comes through the drive-thru and gives you a very long order.

While making the order, you mix up two of the items and make them wrong, but don't realize it. The customer gets very upset and asks to speak to your manager, who criticizes you for the many mistakes you have made since you started working there. How do you respond to their critique?

In this scenario, you're clearly in the wrong because, for whatever reason, you're the one who mixed up some items in the order. Maybe you didn't hear the customer correctly, or maybe you didn't pay attention when you were putting the order together. Either way, you are the one who made the mistake. When your boss confronts you about the mistakes, in addition to the other ones you have made, now is not the time to cower or get defensive. Stand up straight, look them in the eyes, and don't fidget with your hands as they speak to you.

When it's your turn to talk, you could say something like, "I sincerely apologize for my mistake, and I also made sure to apologize to the customer. I take full responsibility, and I will make sure to listen better to ensure I don't make the same mistakes. The speaker was cutting in and out while they were speaking, but I should have asked them to clarify what they said before I started working on their order. I appreciate you taking the time to point out what I have done wrong, and I will work hard to make sure it doesn't happen again."

Notice how there weren't any excuses made? There wasn't an "I'm sorry, I don't know what happened" or "I'm still in training, how was I supposed to know?" Yes, you may have said that the speaker was cutting in and out, but afterward, you acknowledged and took responsibility for your mistake of not asking the customer to repeat the order or reading it back to them to make sure you got it right. Bosses don't like excuses because it tells them that you aren't willing to take accountability when you're wrong. Everyone makes mistakes at work, even your parents, but you must own up to them.

Scenario 2

The holiday season is always very busy, and you have been working long hours at a big brand store. Before your break, you're told to take out the tray in the cash register and put it in the safe; and when you get back from break, you're to go to a different register. Your break was scheduled at the same time as another employee, and when you get back, you accidentally grab the wrong tray.

At the end of the night, the count on your tray is $200 short. Your boss gets suspicious of the missing amount and asks if you stole the money or gave a customer the wrong amount of change back. The amount missing is a large amount, so if you don't figure out what happened, then you will lose your job. What do you do?

Missing money, especially a large amount, can be stressful. You could lose your job or be accused of stealing. However, if you know you double-checked the customer's change and how much they gave you, then you have done nothing wrong. Don't let yourself get worked up or upset. Simply ask them if they could recount your tray. Confidently explain to them you had double-checked the change you gave customers, and perhaps during the shifts change, you switched trays with someone else, as the trays were all kept in the same place. You could even recommend that they count the tray of the same person who went on break at the same time you did. There is no point in crying or hyperventilating because you might lose your job, instead, give options for what could have happened.

You could say something like, "I know the amount of money missing is a lot, but I assure you, I did nothing wrong. I always count the change back twice and do the same thing when I put the money in my drawer. There are other ways this could have happened, and I'm sure we can figure it out together."

Don't allow yourself to stress out because that tells your boss you may have done something wrong but are too afraid to admit it. Instead, be confident, maintain eye contact, and tell them you have no issue figuring out what happened together.

Telling Your Boss "No"

There may be times when your boss asks you to do something that you're unable to do because of work restrictions. If you recall, we covered the importance of saying "No" to your boss in chapter 3 and what it should entail. Read over the next couple of scenarios and think about what you would tell your boss in these situations.

Scenario 1

Although it's Spring Break, the state you live in only allows you to work until 11 p.m. if you're a high school student. The boss tells you that upper management is coming in the next day, and he wants the entire store cleaned from top to bottom. He also says he doesn't care how long it takes; nobody is leaving until it's done. The store is huge and only five employees work that night, so that means you will be there way past the allotted time.

You approach your boss, who already seems on edge, to talk to them. What do you say?

In this situation, your boss is definitely wrong. He knows the laws and overlooks them, so a certain job can be done. Maybe he's angry that other employees haven't been cleaning properly or nervous about dealing with his own boss. Either way, it's not your responsibility to make him feel better.

When you approach him, you could say something like, "I understand that the store needs to be cleaned, but I cannot stay the entire time to finish this job. I only have a half-hour left on my shift, and the law says I'm not allowed to work past 11, even if I'm on Spring Break. I'm willing to work until 11 if you need me, but I can't work past that time." In this situation, you're giving your boss a firm "No," but you're giving a reason behind it in a respectful way. You're reminding them of the law, and even compromising with them a little bit by telling them you will help out until that time. Bringing the law to his attention reminds him that it's out of your hands, but you don't mind doing your part while you're there.

Scenario 2

Tonight's the night of state finals, and you're excited about the big game. Moments before you get ready to leave for the game, your boss calls you and tells you they're short-staffed tonight. They ask you if you can come in, but you tell them about the game, and that you had requested the night of the game off to ensure you didn't have to work or get called in. Your employer gets angry with you because you told them during the interview that you could come in if you're needed. What do you say to them in this situation?

This scenario can be a little tricky because while you told them during the interview you could come in if they were short-staffed, but you also told them about your game schedule and requested the night off. Keep in mind that while your boss is depending on you to come in, you have previous obligations to your teammates who are depending on you to show up as well.

Even though you might be on the phone, your voice can still give your boss some insight into how you're feeling. Don't waver or stutter because that will make them think that you're nervous or questioning whether you can swing going to work instead of going to the game. This opens the door to them asking you to come in again. Instead, say something like, "I understand you need help tonight, but I can't come in. I requested the day off because I have a game. I know that you're depending on me to show up, but so is my team. So, I apologize, but I'm unable to work tonight."

While you are giving them a hard "No," you're still reminding them you have previous obligations and went through the proper channels to ensure that you had the night off.

Dealing With Angry and Rude Customers

A rude, cranky, or angry customer can ruin a good shift. Especially when it's a new job; a disgruntled customer can be extremely unnerving, making you freeze in fear because you don't know what to do. I'm sure by now you have heard the statement, "The customer is always right." However, that isn't always true. Occasionally, a customer thinks that if they are aggressive and make a scene, it will get them what they want. Luckily, with good customer service and assertiveness skills, you can handle whatever gets thrown at you.

Here are a couple of scenarios that will test your customer service techniques.

Scenario 1

This is your first week working at the drive-thru window of a local food chain restaurant, and so far, all your customers are pleased with your service. However, a woman who has just gotten her food pulls back around and yells at you because her food is cold. She demands that you give her a full refund and remake her food. What do you do?

Although the woman is making her wants known, she's going about it all wrong. Her tone of voice and her words might make you shutter, but she's doing so on purpose. She wants you to do what she wants, and she wants you to do it now. While you could remake her food or give her a refund, you can't do both. To counteract her yelling, be sure to speak to her in a calm and relaxed voice. Don't waver or she will keep screaming at you, thinking that if she keeps getting louder than you, you will give her what she wants.

Instead, you could have her pull up to the window and say something like, "I apologize that your food is cold, ma'am. I understand that you would like a full refund and for us to remake your food, however, we're unable to do that. I could either give you your money back or we could remake your food, doing both isn't an option. What can I do to make your experience better?"

Rather than getting snotty or returning the woman's attitude, you're taking control of the situation. You kept a calm tone, showing her that she will not get you to give in to her demands, and you gave her two options before asking how you could make it up to her. If she continues to act belligerent, you have the right to get your boss and have them deal with the customer.

Scenario 2

It's the day before Thanksgiving, and you're working as a cashier at a local grocery store. Three cashiers called off today, leaving only you and one other cashier to tackle the long lines of customers with carts full of last-minute ingredients. Although many of the customers don't mind waiting a few minutes to be checked out, there's one person who seems to be in a rush and doesn't appreciate the lines wrapping all the way around to the aisles. They keep making statements about how it shouldn't take this long and screaming at you and the other cashier to hurry. You can tell their attitude and behavior are getting to the other cashier, and it's causing you to make mistakes as you try to rush.

When it's finally their turn, you notice a scowl on their face as they place their items on the counter. What do you say to them to diffuse the situation?

Before you say anything to the customer, you're going to want to give them a big smile. Although they were being rude, and it's hard to fake a smile with people being so cranky and demanding, remember that your job is to provide your customers with the best service possible. Hopefully, giving them a smile will give them a second to think before they yell at you, and you can say something like, "I'm sorry for your wait, sir. We're doing our best to provide every customer with the best service possible. Do you have any coupons you would like to use today? If not, I have some at the register that will take a few dollars off your items."

By apologizing for their wait and reminding them that every customer has the right to proper service, you're showing them that the people they were waiting behind deserve your attention just as much as they do. You're then offering them coupons if they don't have any readily available that could save them some money, and nothing makes people happier than saving money.

Scenario 3

They have assigned you to work at the customer service counter at your new job while the normal employee takes their lunch break. It's not your first time working at the counter, but you still aren't very comfortable handling returns just yet. A customer walks up to the counter and sets down an item that they would like to return. The date on the receipt abides by the 30-day satisfaction return guarantee. However, you notice the item is warped and has clearly been used multiple times since they purchased it. For this item, the store could not refund or replace the item because it was obviously used and damaged. When you tell the customer that you're unable to take the item back, they get angry with you and demand that you do so. What do you do to diffuse this situation?

It's clear in this situation that the customer isn't right and is trying to get one over on the business by getting their money back on something they used. While you could simply point out and refer to the return policy, this will do nothing to fix the situation—especially if their tone and words are making you nervous. Instead, you could look the customer in the eyes and speak to them in a calm yet firm tone as you say, "Ma'am (or sir), I understand that you're not happy with the product and would like to return it; however, I can see that the item was used and is broken. Even though you returned it within the 30-day window, the policy also clearly states that the item has to be unused and contain all of its parts. The store cannot place the item back into inventory, so we won't be able to refund your money or replace it with another item."

Although there isn't anything you can do for them, you have plainly stated in a firm tone that you're unable to do what they want. If they keep getting louder with you, then you can get your boss, or a supervisor, like in the first scenario, and stand beside your boss as they tell the customer the same thing. Unfortunately, you can't do everything a customer asks.

Working a part-time job can be stressful, especially if it's your first job. The hours can be a lot when added to your school and activity schedule. You never know what you may get yourself into, but by using the assertive skills you have learned so far, you can be mentally and emotionally prepared for any situation thrown your way.

(Before moving on, go to chapter 6 in your workbook and complete all the practices.)

Chapter 7

Dating with Assertiveness

When I want a kiss, I will be the one to take it.

–Natalie C. Parker

High school is a very exciting time, especially where dating is concerned. There are also many challenges, such as saying "No" nicely when someone asks for a date and setting boundaries. This is especially true if this is your first relationship, or you have spent most of your life being an introvert. This is one more very important reason for you to learn how to be an assertive teen. Some romantic partners may try to take up all your time, become needy, and may even become jealous if you spend time with other friends. There will be times when you will need to feel empowered and have the guts to say "No" to a boyfriend or girlfriend.

Turning Down a Date

You are going to be asked out on a date, probably many. While some of these invites are exciting because you like the potential partner asking you, there will be times that you don't want to go out with the person. You could have several reasons, like you don't know them well, you don't like them in that way, or you're worried about ruining a friendship if the date doesn't go well. While it's understandable that telling the person "No" is hard because you don't want to hurt their feelings or make them feel rejected, it's completely necessary.

If you don't like someone or know them well enough to be comfortable spending time with them alone, why would you want to put yourself in that position? The purpose of dating is to spend quality time with someone you're attracted to and have something in common with. You shouldn't be coerced or guilt-tripped into going out with them if you don't feel that way about the person.

Here are a couple of scenarios to respectfully turn down a date using assertiveness:

Scenario 1

You have known one of your best friends since kindergarten, but lately they have been acting kind of strange around you. They keep flirting with you and sending you silly text messages, hinting about a romantic relationship between the two of you. One day, while you're hanging out playing video games, they ask you if you would like to go on an actual date with them.

Although you like hanging out with the person, you're afraid that if the date goes badly, it could ruin your entire friendship. Plus, you have never thought of them in that way, and aren't sure if you want to be in a romantic relationship with them. They stare at you and wait for your answer with a look of concern and worry on their face. What do you say in response?

These types of situations can be especially hard, considering you have known the person for so long and understand how they react when they're let down or sad. Also, you don't want to hurt their feelings. While you should let them down nice and easy, you should still be firm in your response.

You could tell them something like, "I appreciate you asking me out on a date, but I don't think of you in that way. I enjoy spending time with you, and I don't want to ruin our friendship, but I feel like it may if things didn't work out. I hope you understand." Since you are friends, the last thing you want to do is destroy the relationship. It means a lot to you, but you can't allow that to determine whether the relationship progresses to the next stage.

Scenario 2

You have been in a relationship with your boyfriend or girlfriend for a few months now but have been spending a lot of time with your science lab partner. You're thinking they have a crush on you, and one day, they ask you out on a date. How do you respond?

You see this person every day in class, which gives you a reason to let them down firmly, but still nicely. Chances are they didn't know that you are already in a relationship. However, if they knew, they may lack the necessary boundaries to know what they're asking is inappropriate. Either way, you should make sure to maintain eye contact and respond in a firm voice, so they know there's no chance that you will change your mind.

You could say something in the form of, "Thank you for asking me out, but I can't go on a date with you because I'm already in a relationship." That is all you need to say. You don't have to be blunt or mean like telling them you don't think they're attractive. However, you're giving them a reason behind your "no" while keeping your words simple and direct.

Dating and Setting Boundaries

When you first start dating, it's exciting. You're getting to know someone that you like on a whole new level, which can be a good thing and a bad thing. The good part is you have someone else in your corner, someone to spend time with that you enjoy being with, who's there for you on good days and bad. But you also see a side of them the rest of the world doesn't see. You notice their insecurities, see them at their worst, and how they react to different situations.

While the negatives can be a chance for both of you to grow together as individuals, it can also stifle you if your partner lacks the boundaries and self-awareness to recognize their problems and decide to work on them. That's why setting boundaries with your romantic partners is so important.

Nobody wants a boyfriend or girlfriend who's constantly calling or dropping by when you're spending time with your friends or family. Just as it might make you uncomfortable to display your affection in public, but they continue to do so. Talking about how you feel about these topics and where your boundaries lie works best if they're brought up at the very beginning of your relationship. This lets your boyfriend or girlfriend know what you find appropriate, and what you're uncomfortable doing. Of course, you don't have to go over every topic under the sun. Some situations you can talk about when and if they happen. All that's important is that you use your voice if they do something that makes you uncomfortable or feels unsafe, so they don't do it again, and they know what will happen if they continue to act a certain way or do certain things.

Here are a few scenarios that can give you some insight into situations where boundaries with your boyfriend or girlfriend will come in handy.

Scenario 1

You have been in a relationship with your partner for nearly a year, and things are going great except for one not-so-small thing. Whenever you want to hang out with your friends, they throw a fit. When they know you're busy doing something with people other than them, they call and text you constantly, and get angry when you don't respond right away. There have been a couple of times that they followed you and confronted you about not answering their calls, embarrassing you in front of your friends, and causing a scene in a room full of strangers. You find their behavior unacceptable and kind of scary, and your friends keep telling you to break up with them. You have brushed them off in the past, promising to talk to your boyfriend/girlfriend, but it happens again. How do you handle the situation?

Scenarios like this can be scary. Feeling controlled by a partner who's needy for your attention and affection is not a situation anybody wants to be in, and sadly, it can escalate quickly into other, much worse scenarios. If your partner is jealous of your relationship with others, that's an insecurity within themselves, but that doesn't give them the right to control you. You're allowed to have relationships with your friends and family members without them being around.

You might see it as endearing at first, thinking that they just want to spend time with you because they love you so much. But this behavior shows that your partner does not accept your personal rights, and they don't respect you.

You should seriously consider re-evaluating your relationship and decide if you want to continue with it. If you decide to remain in the relationship and work on their behavior together, you could sit them down and firmly state your grievances.

Say something like "I understand you like to spend time with me, but your controlling behavior is completely unacceptable. You make me feel unsafe and intrude on my time with others. I enjoy spending time with my friends and family, just as I enjoy spending time with you, but you don't get to dictate who I spend my time with or when. If you keep acting this way, I will have to end this relationship." In a perfect world, this conversation will do the trick, but often, people who act this way don't see an error in their ways and the absurdity will continue to escalate.

Scenario 2

Your new partner enjoys public displays of affection (PDA), but you find it uncomfortable. You have tried to tell them you don't mind hugging and holding hands when you're out in public but prefer not to make out or have their hands all over you. However, they continue to act this way, sometimes even in front of your parents. What do you say to your new partner, so they can understand how uncomfortable this makes you?

This is the type of situation that could have easily been nipped in the bud with a discussion early in the relationship. However, if you have had this talk, and they continue to do it, assert yourself and remind them of your boundaries.

You could say something like, "I told you when we first started dating that I don't feel comfortable with PDA, but you continue to push me into these things. When you do this, it makes me feel you aren't respecting my boundaries or me. If you keep behaving this way and ignoring my feelings, I will not hang out with you in public anymore. If you have a problem with my decision, we can end the relationship now." Here you have told them what you find acceptable, how it makes you feel, and what the consequences will be if they continue to make you feel uncomfortable. Now, the ball is in their court on how they want to move forward.

Scenario 3

Lately, you have noticed that your partner has been bossy. They have always been blunt and open with their opinion, but in the last few weeks, they have started to tell you what to do, how to dress, and correct you whenever you say something. When you don't follow along with what they want you to do, they get angry and say that you don't care about their feelings. What do you say to them to get them to understand you don't like them bossing you around?

If you recall, when you read over the Personal Bill of Rights section, you have the right to make your own decisions. You have control over your life, and nobody may tell you how to feel, act, think, or behave. After re-evaluating your relationship, you need to have a serious talk with your partner.

You could say something like, "I find your controlling behavior completely unacceptable. I have every right to be myself, and I thought you liked me for me. When you try to change me and boss me around, you make me feel small and unimportant, and that's not the type of relationship I want to be in. If you don't stop acting this way, I have no other choice but to end our relationship."

Here you're making your feelings known, how it makes you feel, and the consequences if things don't change. Hopefully, your partner gets the point and stops bossing you around, but if not, stick to your guns. If you don't follow through, you're only giving them permission to continue treating you like a doormat.

Scenario 4

Recently, you have been spending a lot of time with your partner, and it has been distracting you from your obligations at home, work, and school. It has even taken your attention away from spending time with your family, which you notice is taking a toll on your relationship with your parents and siblings. Last week, you forgot to study for your English exam because you were too busy spending time with your partner. You realize you need to cut back on the time you spend with them and get your life back on track. How do you approach this situation?

Your relationship with your partner isn't the only priority in your life. Your schoolwork, family, and activities should be on your list as well. Recognizing you need to make a change is a good step because you're putting yourself first. You should talk to your partner and let them know your intentions clearly by saying something like, "We have been spending a lot of time together, and it has been distracting me from my other obligations. This doesn't mean we can't hang out, but we need to figure out a time that doesn't interfere with school and spending time with my family." Here you have let your feelings be known and have given them a plan on how to make time for all your priorities.

When Things Go Too Far

We briefly discussed sexual activity between teens in chapter 3, but I feel it's important to bring it up again with some realistic scenarios.

Scenario 1

Although you and your boyfriend or girlfriend have discussed being intimate, you don't feel comfortable being in that type of relationship yet. You have told them this on multiple occasions, but they still keep trying to push your boundaries, and it hurts your feelings that they aren't listening to you. They have even tried to guilt you into going further by saying you don't love them if you won't do this with them. What do you say in response?

As stated before, you have every right to say "No" whenever you don't want to do something. You don't even have to give them a reason. No means no, especially on these occasions. Your partner needs to accept this answer, and if they don't listen to you, then they don't deserve to be with you.

Scenario 2

You and your partner have been intimate occasionally, but after the last time, you decided you aren't comfortable being sexually active any longer. You're afraid to tell your partner, worried that they will break up with you; but when they bring up the conversation about doing it again, you feel it's time to let them know how you feel. What do you tell them, so they understand how you're feeling?

The answer to this is much simpler than it sounds. If they don't respect that you're no longer okay being intimate with them, then they don't respect you, your rights, or your boundaries. How you decide to tell them is up to you, but make sure you tell them why you don't want to, and what you need from them, mainly their support and respect for your decision.

The point is, you have the choice of how quickly or slowly, and how far your relationship goes. Nobody may take that control from you, even if you feel you love them. Someone who controls you, bosses you around, pushes your boundaries, and makes you feel unsafe doesn't love you—because that's not love. Whether it's a friend or a boyfriend/girlfriend, they need to respect the rules you have made for yourself and encourage you to follow them. If they don't, then you have every right to discontinue the relationship, feeling no guilt.

Conclusion

When you first picked this book up, you may have had a hard time imagining the day when you would feel confident in every social situation. As you continue to practice the skills you have learned your life will slowly develop into one where you feel comfortable with yourself and others, confident in your ability to make your wants and needs effectively heard, and any anxiety that you may have had in the past should improve.

As you continue to grow, use the tools you have learned here to continue on to a lifelong path of self-discovery, which will keep you in control of your life's trajectory and propel you toward your dreams. You should continue to self-reflect anytime you feel unsure about a situation. This will keep you true to yourself and your values. You will also want to review your list of values and your Personal Bill of Rights from time to time, because as you grow as a person, these things may change. Something that is important to you in high school, like being the most popular, may change as you move into your role as an adult. For example, in life, most people come to realize that the opinions of others have little value to them.

Over time, your personal boundaries may change as well. Remember that things are not set in stone, and you have every right to adjust them as you see fit. One thing that will remain with you is your new ability to assert your own values, rights, and boundaries in all aspects of your life. This skill will be invaluable to you as you move into adulthood and navigate your career, find a life partner, and someday, perhaps, raise your own family. You will always need assertive communication because there will always be authority figures, family members, and people with no sense of boundaries to deal with.

One thing is for sure, knowing that you can control your part in all your relationships will lead to a greater sense of happiness and satisfaction in your life. Living a life based on your values will help you steer yourself in the right direction to get what you want from life. This is going to give you better self-esteem, less guilt, and reduced anxiety.

Now that you have reached the end, I truly hope that you found this book to be informative and helpful. I hope that I have equipped you to push past any fears and insecurities that have previously stopped you from standing up for yourself. I hope that I have provided you with a better sense of control over your life and given you the tools to take charge.

If you also used the workbook, then you have had lots of practice opportunities by now. I suggest you keep it, because there are many areas where you can continue to use the workbook to prepare for life situations. If you continue to practice and attempt to keep improving, you'll find that soon you no longer need the workbook because these things will become second nature to you.

Now, get out there and assume the role of CEO in your life!

If you found this book and workbook to be helpful, I hope you will take a moment to leave a review on Amazon or Kindle. Reviews really help authors like me to reach more people and help others like yourself.

Thank you for choosing Social Skills Teens Need to Survive High School.

www.Amazon.com/dp/B0BQ99WJSC

www.EtheriaPublishing.com

Etheria Publishing Early Reviewer Program

Visit https://etheriapublishing.com/early-reviewers-program/

References

1. Ackerman, C. E. (2017, December 18). 87 Self-Reflection Questions for Introspection. Positive Psychology. https://positivepsychology.com/introspection-self-reflection/

2. Assertive Communication—6 Tips for Effective Use. (n.d.). Impact Factory. https://www.impactfactory.com/resources/assertive-communication-6-tips-for-effective-use/

3. Assertiveness. (2019). Psychology Today. https://www.psychologytoday.com/us/basics/assertiveness

4. Baird, A. (2017, August 14). Assertive Body Language. Sensei. https://sensei.ie/assertive-body-language/

5. Barkley, S., & Currin-Sheehan, K. (2022, September 15). This is How to Set Boundaries With Your Parents. Psych Central. https://psychcentral.com/relationships/setting-boundaries-with-parents#parental-boundaries-are-unique

6. Dani. (2021, August 19). The Importance of Self-Reflection as a Teenager in 2022. Teen Financial Freedom. https://teenfinancialfreedom.com/the-importance-of-self-reflection-as-a-teenager-in-2022/

7. Darcy, A. M. (2019, June 25). 12 Signs You Lack Healthy Boundaries (and Why You Need Them). Harley TherapyTM Blog. https://www.harleytherapy.co.uk/counselling/healthy-boundaries.htm

8. Five Steps to Negotiating With Parents and Carers. (n.d.). Young Scot. https://young.scot/get-informed/national/five-steps-to-negotiating-with-parents-and-carers

9. Gordon, S. (2021, July 26). Everything Your Teen Needs to Know About Setting Boundaries. Verywell Family. https://www.verywellfamily.com/boundaries-what-every-teen-needs-to-know-5119428

10. Gordon, S. (2022, March 7). 7 Ways to Improve Assertiveness So You Don't Get Bullied. Verywell Family. https://www.verywellfamily.com/how-teaching-assertiveness-can-prevent-bullying-460681

11. Healthwise. (2017, October 10). Stress Management: Reducing Stress by Being Assertive. Kaiser Permanente. https://wa.kaiserpermanente.org/kbase/topic.jhtml?docId=av2095

12. How to Deal With Annoying, Difficult, and Disrespectful Siblings. (2019, November 25). UpJourney. https://upjourney.com/how-to-deal-with-annoying-difficult-and-disrespectful-siblings

13. The Importance of Knowing & Living Your Values. (2020, July 1). Applied Positive Psychology Learning Institute. https://appli.edu.au/knowing-living-your-values/

14. Jay, C. (2022, September 11). How to Refuse a

Date Gracefully: 12 steps. WikiHow. https://www.wikihow.com/Refuse-a-Date-Gracefully

15. Konter-O'Hara, S. (2022, September 23). Personal Boundaries Quiz. WellMinded Counseling. https://wellmindedcounseling.com/therapist-blog/2016/9/5/personal-boundaries-quiz

16. McGregor, J. (2017, May 29). How to Be Assertive and Set Healthy Boundaries. Welldoing. https://welldoing.org/article/how-be-assertive-set-healthy-boundaries

17. Mizrahi, J. (2020, April 27). The Importance of Self-Reflection in Learning. Today's Learner. https://todayslearner.cengage.com/the-importance-of-self-reflection-in-learning

18. Panayotova, L. (2015, December 22). Personal Bill of Rights. Explorable. https://explorable.com/e/personal-bill-of-rights

19. Self-Reflection 101: What Is Self-Reflection? Why Is Reflection Important? And How to Reflect. (2020). Holstee. https://www.holstee.com/blogs/mindful-matter/self-reflection-101-what-is-self-reflection-why-is-r

eflection-important-and-how-to-reflect

20. Stressed Out? Be Assertive. (2022, May 13). Mayo Clinic. https://www.mayoclinic.org/healthy-lifestyle/stress-management/in-depth/assertive/art-20044644

21. Teaching Teens Self-Reflection. (2018, February 18). Los Angeles Teen Therapist. https://losangelesteentherapist.com/create-a-better-experience-of-life-through-self-reflection

22. TeensHealth. (2015). Talking to Your Parents—or Other Adults (For Teens). Kidshealth. https://kidshealth.org/en/teens/talk-to-parents.html

23. Truett, S. (2018, July 2). How to Say No Effectively: A Guide for Teenagers and Other People. Relationship Builders. https://relationshipbuilders-lakeland.com/say-no-effectively-guide-teenagers-people/

24. Vavrichek, S. M. (2013, January 28). How to Be Assertive While Keeping a Kind Heart. PsychAlive. https://www.psychalive.org/how-to-be-assertive-while-keeping-a-kind-heart/

25. Violen, J. (2022, October 24). Social Skills: Promoting Positive Behavior, Academic Success, and School Safety. NASP Center. https://naspcenter.org/factsheets/social-skills/

26. Whyte, A. (2018, April 23). How to Help Your Teen Set Healthy Dating Boundaries. Evolve Treatment Centers. https://evolvetreatment.com/blog/healthy-dating-boundaries/

Printed in Great Britain
by Amazon